Babyland:

Memoirs of a Sugar Daddy

Blake Gold

Contents

FORWARD-

So, what's a sugar baby? I didn't know but I was soon going to learn that it's addictive, fun, dangerous, but definitely not a positive influence on family, work, or health. But did I mention that it's fun lol. That's one thing you learn quickly in babyland. Text short hand and emojis.

My first baby wasn't really a baby per se. She was/is a porn star. Let's say this. My learning curve regarding babyland was steep and I quickly hiked up the mountain and then, just as quickly fell, down into a very deep valley. But then I was resurrected. That's a big part of babyland. The ups and downs. They are addictive and, of course, destructive.

But I'm getting ahead of myself as I didn't know any of this when as a married, successful professional I booked my first online date with a porn star escort. She had been an online fantasy of mine for a couple years and I thought to myself, "What's the worst that could happen?". Well, I didn't have a clue about the highs and lows that decision would lead to. Loss of a spouse, a job, and almost kids, and a career to boot. All in pursuit of younger women and sex.

This is my story.

1) BB-

Raise your hand if you watch porn?

For those who have, have you ever found that one woman who you wanted to get to know as a person. Someone you could come home to, have kids with, live happily after?

Me neither. So, I booked my date as an escape. An escape from a sexless marriage and a perceived opportunity for pleasure with what I imagined would be a totally well-rounded young woman who had chosen to perform sex on film for money for some good reason and that she would be happy to take my money to make my fantasies come true. How wrong I was.

For background. I was "happily" married. 25 years to the same woman. A beautiful, age-appropriate women who had given me the best years of her life. Under a bonding oath till death (or a really hot, young, fucked up, porn star) do us part.

So, I figured as I moved into a transitional period with my job where I would be placed in a boring position in the US after years of interesting and stimulating overseas work, I figured I could have one last experience that would satiate that lingering curiosity about "sex with a younger woman" before I moved into a never-ending cycle of lawn mowing and taking out the garbage.

And it only cost me $48,000. I guess I should have done some research and I would have learned that it's not necessary to pay that much. But what did I know? I was a starry eyed 55-year-old with fantasies. So, I paid.

But I had to do it in installments so not to lead to questions from my wife. So, I moved some mutual funds around, sent small (and not so small amounts) to a mysterious online company, and then had to hit the banks. Apparently, (another learning point), you can't take out more that 10k at a time from a bank or they have to report it to the IRS. So, I took out 9,999 at multiple banks in NYC thinking at the time I was outsmarting them all. Didn't know why I was getting such knowing looks from the tellers lol... Sorry for the lols but a year and a half with 19-22-year-olds creates some ingrained habits 😌.

I was all set. Under the cover story of visiting my dying mother and finding a house in the US for us to live, I traveled to Miami (what I was to learn is the epicenter of sugar baby/sugar daddy world...) to meet her. Of course, I'm not a complete jerk. I did visit my dying mother and did hire a realtor but I also left a couple days open for my "date".

Being new to this, I figured the bigger and more expensive the better. So, Miami Heat game (second row), waterfront dining, room at W hotel Miami Beach with wraparound balcony with view of the harbor and ocean. Sounded impressive to me but obviously I didn't know her.

In retrospect, I should have known there was something wrong from the beginning. The fact that I was looking at this like a prom date and how she was probably looking at it (and from what she told me later) we were on different pages of different books.

Being an over-organized (mildly OCD individual) I figured the idea of meeting at a hotel, getting a limo ride to a basketball game, watching the game, getting dinner, and then heading back to the hotel wasn't rocket science. But apparently, according to the person I will from now on call BB, it wasn't so simple...

So, part one, meeting at 7pm at the hotel. Phone call, I'm running a little late. Can we meet at the game? Sure. Halftime. Phone call, I'm running a little late. I hope I can get there before the game is over. Ok. Game's over. Ok, I'll meet you back at the hotel at 10. Ok. I'll be there. 2 AM. Phone call. Don't know where I am but I think I'm close.

I get out of bed where I had been comfortably asleep, get dressed, and wait. 3 AM, I think I'm close. Can you come down?

So, I wandered downstairs and through the parking lot and around the corner and then another corner and then straight ahead of me I saw a person getting out of a broken-down light brown dodge dart. She busily fixed her hair and then looked up at me and, when I looked into her eyes, that was the beginning of the end.

I don't know how to explain what I saw in her bright green eyes but I knew from articles about those who had done crack cocaine that they described being instantly addicted. I guess that's how I felt at that moment.

She was short, petite, slim, with light caramel skin. But was most striking was her vulnerability. While she struggled to get her suitcase out of the backseat her top completely fell off leaving her naked from the waist up and, seemingly unaware, she started to wheel her suitcase down the sidewalk toward me.

"Hi," she said, stretching her small and toned arms toward me. Smiling through botox-infiltrated lips she noticed me glancing towards her small breasts, naked in the south Florida moonlight.

"Oh," she laughed. "Guess I need to find my top."

I knew at that point my life would definitely never be the same.

So, I haven't been completely honest. I didn't actually plan to have sex with her. I realize how strange that might seem to spend that much money and not actually consummate the deal but that is how hung up on roles and rules I had become in my life. I at that point somehow believed I would just spend some quality time with her and then I would move on. Back to my life which was following a path destined to include the requisite working until 65, vacations at our condo in Belize and lake house in the Berkshire mountains of Massachusettes, doting over the not yet arrived grandkids and then, finally, segueing into my final resting place, as yet to be determined. Ashes in the ocean or flung off a mountain top; to add to water pollution or global warming, I hadn't yet decided. I had a moral code goddamnit. At least at that point I thought I did.

So, there she was. Still standing there on the sidewalk. I was stunned by the immensity of her being crammed into such a small body. One could see she had experienced so much and yet so little at the same time. It was too much to process at 3 AM, mildly hungover from mini bar vodkas and my own lingering self-pity thinking I had been stood up after spending that much money.

"Hi," I replied, reaching out awkwardly to grab her suitcase.

We walked single file along the pastel-colored pavement, the oranges and yellows and greens glowing under the fluorescent street lamps' glare.

"How was your trip?" I asked into the air in front of me, afraid to look back and see that she was gone, heading back to her car to head back to where ever she had come from, comfortable to leave her suitcase just to not have to spend another night with a man who was paying for her company.

"Long," she replied. Her voice was husky, especially for someone so small, but it completed the package.

"Oh," I stopped and turned toward her. "Can I carry take the bag for you?" I asked, still unclear about the rules of this interaction.

"That's so sweet," she replied. I was trying to figure out her accent.

"Where are you from?" I asked as I reached for her suitcase and pulled it from behind her.

"Savannah."

"Georgia?"

"Of course, silly."

There was something so disarming about her and our seemingly innocent banter that I didn't watch where I was going and nearly got hit by a car making a right hand turn as I stepped off the curb. She ran up to me and grabbed my hand.

"Sweetie, are you ok?"

I looked into those bright green eyes again and was instantly healed.

"Yes," I replied, continuing to walk, now turning the corner and entering the hotel grounds.

At this point I realized that the few people lingering outside the hotel at this hour were staring at her and then by association at me. I hadn't really imagined how this would play out and now that it was happening, I'm sure it looked like exactly what it was. An older man with a young porn star prostitute. All of a sudden, I wasn't sure what to do. Was this illegal? Were they going to block my entrance? Were they going to call the cops and make a scene?

I slowed down to allow her to catch up to me and as we walked through the lobby, past the front desk, and toward the elevator, I realized that while everyone was looking at us, I was only getting supportive looks and knowing smiles. Well, this is interesting I thought to myself as the elevator door opened and an older gentleman exited and then made a point of holding the door open for us and giving me a thumbs up as the door closed behind us.

"What a beautiful view!" BB exclaimed while standing on the balcony, smoking a cigarette, and craning her neck to see in all directions.

I should add at this point that she was completely naked and seemingly very comfortable. I am not sure when she had the opportunity to get her clothes off from the time we entered the room to the time we got to the balcony but somehow she had managed without my noticing.

So, you want to know what a porn star looks like in person? I definitely was unsure how much was real and how much was video enhanced, edited, or otherwise altered. All I can say in BB's case she was more beautiful, sensual, and sexual in person than I could have imagined. Her hair flowed in curly waves down her tanned and toned shoulders, her back muscles were taut, her butt was rounded but firm and her legs were perfectly defined as she raised up on her toes to look farther out over the ocean.

"Do you think I can sit on the railing?" she asked as she started to push herself up with her arms.

I jumped off my chair and grabbed her around the waist as her feet raised off the ground and pulled her away from the ledge.

"What are you doing?!" I asked incredulously.

"Just having fun," she replied innocently and then grabbed my hand and led me into the bedroom.

"Sorry baby but I have to ask…" her small voice trailed off and was difficult to hear over the sound of the waves breaking beyond the balcony.

"Oh," I replied finally understanding and went to my bag to get the 10k that I was told I would have to give her.

"Thanks honey," she purred as she silently scanned the contents of the envelope and then slipped it into her purse.

Ok, I'm sure some of you want to know the details about what happened next. Well, I'm not going to tell you. All I will say is it was the most mind blowing, reality altering, erotic, sensual, sexual experience of my life. Lol.

Then we fell asleep. And she snored. A lot. Like a freight train. So, I spent the rest of the night trying to figure out how such a loud noise could emanate from such a small person. The physics were confounding. But she was so beautiful lying there, dreaming of whatever she was dreaming of. And then somehow, I fell asleep, watching her.

I woke up to her sucking my dick. I guess there is no other way to say it. And it was a wonderful way to start the day.

"Good morning," she said, smiling and peeking up from between my legs, after she and I were done.

"Good morning," I replied and pulled her up next to me. I was still amazed at how small she was. She seemed to have read my mind.

"I'm a spinner," she said.

"A what?" I asked.

"A spinner," she said again. "It's what they call small porn stars. And before you ask, I'm 4 foot 11 and 95 pounds.

"Oh," I replied, not really knowing what to say at that point. "Want to take a shower?" I asked.

"Sure," she answered and bounded out of bed into the bathroom and before I knew it, somehow, magically, we were having sex again.

So, Viagra. I know you knew it was going to come up. Yes, I was taking it. And yes, it works. And yes, I took way too much, so my face was red and I had a pounding headache but it was worth it. I think I took 300 mg over the night just to make sure everything continued to work. Who knows if things would have worked anyway but no way for that amount of money and for that experience I going to take the chance?

I didn't mess around with the generic stuff. I had contacted my doctor and made up a story about having tried the generic and it not working. It ended up costing my ten dollars a pill for the brand name but I'm convinced that it worked better. Even it's all psychological it was worth it.

I also had learned with my wife that if you drink you have to take more. A lot more. Like instead of 25 mg I would usually take 100 mg to start. I never had a heart attack from it so I figured I should just titrate to effect.

Anyway, we were clean and post coital.

"Want to go to the pool?" I asked.

"Sure," she replied. "But then I have to go."

I was shocked. "But I paid through tomorrow."

"Sorry baby," she replied. "Just tell my agent I didn't show up and you'll get your money back. I will have gotten mine and she will never know," she continued and then sucked from her vape sending a cloud of watermelon flavored smoke swirling around her head.

"I can't do that," I said. "Can I?" I asked, of course being new to this had no idea of the rules."

"You're new to this aren't you?" she asked.

I didn't know what to say so I did what I was trained to do my whole safe role-oriented life. I told the truth.

"Yes."

"I could tell," she replied as she slipped on her what one could call a bathing suit but was mostly just two small strips of cloth with a lot of string. "Ok," she added. "Let's go," and started to skip, literally skip, down the hallway to the door. Damn, I was in trouble.

At the pool things didn't get much more normal. Apparently, people knew who BB was. My first hint was when the pool attendant shyly asked whether she could sign his butt.

"Of course, dear," she replied coyly while he bent over and waited patiently for her to find a pen.

After she signed, she gave him a peck on the cheek and then, surprisingly, he turned to me and said quietly. "You're a lucky guy," and winked before turning back to his towels.

"Let's go to the beach?" she asked while grabbing my hand and pulling me behind her like a puppy.

"Ok," I replied and fell in line behind her very aware of the smiles and glares, from the men and women respectfully, as we headed to the beach area.

Despite the line at the beach attendant station, somehow, magically, the attendant skipped the entire line of wide-eyed, incredulous tourists and came up to BB and asked, "Where would you like to sit?"

"You choose," BB replied coyly and the attendant led us to a pair of chairs just beyond the tide line and quickly picked up the "Reserved" sign and laid out towels on the chairs before turning to BB. "Anything you need just let me know," and then, he bowed. I still was trying to wrap my head around the situation and then realized I needed to tip him. I reached for my wallet but before I could pull out the money the attendant leaned into my ear and said, "You are a lucky man," and pushed the bill back into my hand.

So, this was going to be life with BB.

2) WIFE AND FAMILY-

So. After BB drove away that afternoon and I called to cancel my dinner reservations I had made at Nobu South Beach, I tried to process what had just happened. It was as if my life had completely transformed overnight and I had no idea what to do next. I do know that I felt guilty and so like any good role-oriented person who had been taught to do the right thing… I called my wife to confess.

"Hi," I said softly.

"How's Florida?" she asked. From the background sounds I could tell she was doing the dishes.

"Um," I paused.

"What's wrong?" I could imagine her putting down the sponge.

"Something happened," I said softly.

"What" she replied sounding concerned.

"I had an affair with a porn star and I think I have feelings for her."

It's been a couple years and I realize in retrospect that was not the way to have handled the situation. But at that point in time, bathed in starry-eyed infatuation, I wasn't aware.

"Don't come home," she replied. "And go to sex rehab," she added before hanging up.

Sex rehab? I asked myself. At the time I didn't even know what that was.

Well, I continued the conversation with myself, I guess if I want to go home, I need to find out. Like a good husband who had done something wrong, and was trying to please his wife I searched for sex rehabs.

To be honest I had never heard of sex rehab but apparently, it's a big industry in the US currently.

Tiger Woods, Harvey Weinstein, Kevin Spacey, just some of the rich and famous who have spent time at them is what I learned from a quick internet search. But was I a sex addict? I had no idea but since my wife told me I had to go to get our marriage back I was going to go.

So, after some phone calls and very invasive questioning by well-meaning intake specialists I decided to go the Ranch in Tennessee. Thankfully I was due for some vacation time so I put in for a couple weeks and within a few days I was there.

I think my story was confusing to them but when I arrived, I felt like I belonged. Although it wasn't what I imagined. No famous people or 5-star meals. Mostly a bunch of men who had mistook sex for intimacy and had paid the price. Fell in love with cam models, spent thousands on their "girlfriends", or prostitutes or pornsites, whatever the vice, I felt like I understood what they were missing and were searching for with their misguided attempts.

But after a week I was done, and then, thankfully my mom died. So, I had an excuse to escape. I know that sounds terrible but I had no relationship with my mother so her death was a get out of jail card. And so, the circumstances granted me a three-day pass to deal with her funeral with the expectation I would return and complete the 30-day program. But that was not my plan…

And then somehow, I ended up in Nashville with the police knocking on my door.

I didn't think anything was off but that is the thing about being in the throes of addiction. You don't know you are. Well, nothing to make you realize that's where you are than to have three heavily armed police officers doing a safety check on you while you are just enjoying a nice evening of perusing porn videos online and the availability of local escorts. It definitely sobers you up. Especially when you realize your adult children were concerned enough about you to track you down and call the police to your hotel room.

After that experience I realized I needed to take this all more seriously.

So, I upped my game. As most addicts do, I decided to go all in. I researched the best sex rehab in the US and made a reservation. The Meadows in Arizona. That is where many of the best know sex addicts went for treatment so I figured they could sort me out. Rewire me or whatever they do in places like that and then I could go back to my life.

3) Meadows-

The Gentle Path. That's what the sex rehab program is called at the Meadows in Arizona. I have had some time since going there to think about that name and I'm still not sure how I feel about it. It's definitely a path, however, there is no way it is gentle.

Most sex addicts have issues regarding intimacy and love that were created early in life through dysfunctional and/or abusive relationships with those who were supposed to have cared about them. They look at sex as giving them what they crave, that lost connection and intimacy. So, the idea that that type of dysfunction and psychopathology will be fixed in 45 days, for a cool 40 thousand dollars (insurance not accepted) is not really a practical reality. But I went anyway.

In retrospect it was like a male adult summer camp for men who had lost their way or had never found it, in respect to the societal norms regarding sex, and money, and intimacy. I learned about terms like "Findom" which is financial dominance, where essentially a man controls a woman through his money even if there is no sex connected. Men who had spent tens of thousands on webcam models, prostitutes, and sugar babies all told their stories. All in search of connection that they were deprived of as children.

I, of course, came in with my story, "happily married" for 25 years. Three kids, all functional and happy, and then the slowly boiling pot of insecurity boiled over and led to an affair with a porn star who I then fell quickly and completely in love with. I felt like I belonged.

Until about day 30…. Then I was done. The psychobabble could not compete with the yearning and I started to count my days to discharge. Pocketing my meds in my mouth and then spitting them out, telling the therapists what I knew they wanted to hear, realizing that this was not the approach that was going to "heal" me. So, I played ping pong, corn hole, water volleyball watching the circling planes of paparazzi above our heads trying to shoot the next pic for National Enquirer. I did the neurofeedback, EMDR therapy attempting to de-lateralize my dysfunctional brain, acupuncture, all for naught.

The first thing I did when I pulled out of the gates and they gave me my phone was to text BB and tell her I was out and wanted to meet her back in Florida. And then things got bad.

4) BB REDUX-

So, I had a top-secret security clearance and a job which required it. My lawyers tell me that's all I can reveal.

My plan was to bring BB on a work trip overseas and tuck her away in hotel while I did my business and would come back to her with no one the wiser every evening.

Well, I should have listened to them.

On a lovely day BB and I boarded an American Airlines flight from Miami to Bermuda. As I sat next to her in high heels, fishnet stockings, and an almost non-existent top, I thought to my deluded self, "This seems fine. Not sure what everyone was worried about."

And then the shitstorm arrived.

I should have seen the signs. The looks from the stewardess as she passed us walking up the aisle. The questions about why BB was sleeping. My explanation that she was tired after a long drive to the airport. When the same conversation happened a few times and the looks became more antagonist, I, even in my mildly inebriated state (I was chatting with a British expat in the aisle seat about whatever the world issue was of the moment) realized there was something going on.

So maybe in retrospect I shouldn't have been surprised when the pilot announced that there would be a delay on the tarmac.

And then when we got off the plane and were directed to the front of the customs and immigration line, I thought it was just the usual VIP treatment which I had been accustomed to. Only when the questions started about why I was in the country and who my friend was I realized this was not the red-carpet treatment I was expecting.

I was fucked. I knew that when I saw BB semi-naked in the waiting room outside where I was being interrogated.

"I need to call the Embassy," I said quietly, suddenly recognizing my situation.

"Ok", the Bermuda officer replied stoically, and gave me back my phone.

Suddenly an American Customs and Border patrol agent barged in and said I needed to talk to him and he dragged me out of the office.

"Do you know what they think you did?" he asked.

"No idea," I replied.

"They think you sex trafficked her into the country," he said quietly.

"Why would they think that?"

"Apparently the stewardess thought you met the profile of a sex trafficker based on a course that she took last week."

I didn't really know what to say at that point.

"And she was found carrying drugs," he added.

"Shit," I said to myself.

"Do you want to talk with her?" he asked.

I could tell he was trying to be helpful and knew the situation looked bad.

"Thanks."

He left and brought BB into the room and he stepped out quietly.

"Scott," she started crying. "I'm so sorry."

"You know they think I was sex trafficking you?" I asked.

"No fucking way!" She exclaimed.

"But that's not our biggest problem," I added. "Did you have drugs on you?"

She paused. "Yes," she started, "but I thought Bermuda was still part of the United States."

"Well, it's not," I said, "and we're fucked."

Just then a Bermuda Border patrol official came in and told BB to come with him.

"Scott, please don't let them take me!" She cried out as he grabbed her arm and led her out of the room.

Just then I could see everyone in the office area stand at attention and salute. The door swung open and a tall woman wearing a classy beige pantsuit entered the room.

"I'm the Ambassador," she said and then sat down. "So quite a mess," she added looking me directly in the eyes. "I have been briefed and we can get you out of the country by invoking diplomatic immunity but not sure what we can do for your…. friend." She stopped but continued to stare at me.

"I'm sorry you were dragged into this," I replied. Her gaze did not waver and it was unnerving.

She clapped her hands together abruptly and I jumped. "Well let's see what we can do about all this," and she sprung up and headed out the door, not waiting for me to follow.

Outside, I struggled to keep up with her and the two Embassy security guards who flanked her on both sides and the Bermuda officer they were following.

Soon we turned a corner and there was BB in the middle of the floor of a large room with a handful of officers surrounding her. She was curled in a fetal position, sobbing, and when she saw us enter, she jumped up and ran over to me.

"Scott," she said while trying to wipe the tears away, "they say I'm going to jail."

I turned to the Ambassador. "Is there anything we can do for her?" I asked softly. And then added in a whisper, "She has a lot of mental health issues and I'm really worried about her safety."

The Ambassador regarded me stoically and then glanced briefly at BB before heading over to one of the Bermuda guards. While I couldn't hear what they were saying I could tell the Ambassador was pleading her case and negotiating some sort of deal.

She headed back to us. "They say you can take responsibility for her for the night at a hotel nearby and that you both have to fly out in the morning." And she added, "You both will never be allowed to return to Bermuda."

"Thank you so much," BB cried and went to hug her but the Ambassador quickly put out her hand and BB shook it weakly.

The Ambassador turned to me. "This will be a problem for your career you realize."

I hadn't really thought about the situation and how it would impact me until that moment but suddenly I realized I was likely going to be looking for a new job.

5) Back in the USA-

After a challenging trip back to the USA: BB was upset they took her passport on arrival back to the States for some unclear reason and almost got arrested for yelling at the US customs officer, the fact she kept passing out (snorting fentanyl?), and almost not being able to get on the last connecting flight due to her having to be semi-carried onto the plane, we finally arrived back in Florida.

And as expected it was only a few days before I was called to Washington DC for "consultations". Consultations is a euphemism for "you're in a shitload of trouble."

So off I headed to DC to meet my union supplied lawyer (who was not optimistic when I shared the details of the Bermuda experience) and then the Diplomatic security team that would review the situation.

First, I had the unpleasant experience of walking into my main office and having people staring at me like I had just taken a porn star on a work trip…. Background, during my 10 years in the organization I had been perceived as being a solid, reliable, responsible, probably boring employee and suddenly I was not. And while I knew it was likely going to result in me losing my job it did feel freeing in a way. As if all of those expectations had immediately and irrevocably been blown up. I had always struggled with being the "good boy" and now I wasn't.

So, I went through the expected interrogation by my immediate supervisor, the deputy director, and even the director came in to quickly judge and convict me. I would say that it was uncomfortable and I was sorry for the stain I was told I imparted on the department but, in all truth, I'm sure more people were entertained by the tale rather than actually enraged.

That was followed then by a fun filled day of spilling my secrets to two young men in black suits who were old enough to be my son. I could see them struggle to believe the fact that this was now their task. To somehow decide whether someone who had obviously had a severe lapse in judgement should allowed to handle top secret national information.

I wanted to cut it short and tell them the answer should be "no" and walk out of the office and move on with my life. But again, I was entertained by the questions and their responses, both verbal and not, to my answers. "So where did you meet," one paused, "this BB?" "Online," I replied. "And you're saying that you guys were dating?" the other asked, trying to stifle his judgement. "Yes." "Well, we did some research and she's a pretty famous porn star," the one paused (I stifled a chuckle about what his research involved and what his wife would say if she caught him). "Why would a well-known porn star want to date you?" And they both stared at me." I then went ahead and explained Sugarbaby 101 to them. I'm sure by doing so I was sealing my fate however the looks they gave me were worth it. "So," the one said, "you actually believe you two are a couple." "Yes," I replied before they moved onto other questions regarding my decision making and judgement which I believe I passed but I knew by the way they were asking the questions they had already made their decision.

And in a few days, it was confirmed. In a tersely worded email, I was informed that my security clearance had been revoked and that I should discuss further steps with my supervising department. At that point it was just a matter of time before I retired as I knew it would be impossible to do my job overseas without a clearance and there was no way I was going to wander the halls of the DC government building looking for some pointless presentation to give or some useless policy to develop. So, while my retirement paper work was being processed I decided to have some fun in DC.

At that point in my experiences I, in retrospect, hadn't really experienced much in the world of commercial sex. Never had been to a strip club let alone hired a prostitute. But I figured at this point since the die had been cast what was the worst that could happen? I did realize that getting arrested wouldn't be great but at that point I was fueled on adrenaline of finally being free from the perceived bonds of marriage and career expectations.

Where to find a prostitute? That was my question. Couldn't ask a friend or family member so I turned to the internet. And before I knew it, I was on listcrawler and escortfinder and a variety of other sites where, after weeding through the obvious frauds one could find a sexual experience for about 300-500 dollars an hour. So off I went. During the days I continued to play the bureaucratic games, but at 5 I would head off on alcohol and Viagra filled evenings in random hotel rooms throughout the city. It was fun and exciting and in my mind at that time, even a little dangerous. That feeling of that hotel room door opening and not being sure if it would be a cop or a couple guys ready to beat me up and rob me. But still I persisted. Then I decided I still wasn't satisfied so I hired someone to live with me at my temporary apartment. It was perfect. For 2000 she stayed with me for the last three days of my time in DC. I would give her a kiss (or get a blowjob) before heading off to "work" and then we would hit the bars and restaurants of DC until late in the night when we would stumble home, have sex, and then the cycle would repeat. I remember thinking how I could live like this long term. I mean other than the looks we would get (she was a 25-year-old tall black woman who wore very few clothes and had an amazing body) and the dent in my bank account, I didn't really see the downside.

So, now retired, and free of any job or relationship commitment, with some cash from separating from government employment, I headed back to the country's epicenter of sex, drug and alcohol use. South Florida. What could go wrong?

6) Crazy B-

Looking back, this is when I dove, head first, into sugar daddy world. I don't know when I first heard the term, probably on one of the dating sites I started trying out around that time. First was the obvious, Tinder. At the time I thought it was a hook up site but I quickly learned that if you matched with someone under 30 and you were in your fifties, they wanted a "financially beneficial relationship", a euphemism for being a sugar baby.

The first woman I met from the site was a seemingly normal 23-year-old, Laura. After a lot of texting and then talking on the phone we decided to meet. But, of course, at that point in my life I couldn't just do a normal meet. She had told me a sob story over the week prior that she had been kicked out of her apartment by her boyfriend, who had broken or thrown away all her stuff and she was living on the streets. So, I naturally said she could come and stay with me for a while. Again, ignoring the rules retrospectively of common sense, I drove south from Ft. Lauderdale where I was living at the time, down to Miami.

Now, over the brief time I had been on Tinder, I knew that people edited their photos to look better than they actually looked. You could learn to tell who was using a filter or editing software to edit out acne, body fat, or any other perceived unattractive feature. However, nothing prepared me for what I saw when I pulled up in front of the building where she suggested we meet.

Instead of the short, thin, perfectly proportioned Icelandic beauty, I found myself staring at short, frumpy, unkempt, overweight woman with greasy black hair and acne scars on her face holding a suitcase and waving frantically. I had a choice at that point obviously, I could follow through on my promise, and give her a place to stay, or I could just drive past. I stopped.

"Hey baby," she said as she climbed into the passenger seat after she threw her suitcase in the back.

"Hey," I replied, not really knowing what to say.

We drove the hour drive making small talk while my brain was trying to figure out how I was going to get out of the situation.

After we arrived in my apartment, I tried to do what usually worked for me when I had a problem. I drank. A lot. But it didn't help enough. I figured I could see what her body looked like so we made out but when I slipped my hand down her shirt she pulled away.

"Let's take it slow baby."

Well, this was getting even more complicated. I knew from what she had told me that she wanted to stay for a month while she found a new place. And at this point I knew there was no way I was going to last more than the night with this new roommate.

After sleeping on the couch and giving up my bed to her I woke with a stiff neck and my dog staring at me.

"I know," I said to her, "I have to get her out of here."

So, after Laura woke, I didn't waste any time telling her she was going to have to leave.

Of course, she started to cry.

"Where am I going to go?" she started to sob. "You promised."

It's true, I did but it's not like there was a contract.

"How about I get you a place for a couple days?"

"Ok," she replied, the tears slowing.

So, after finding her an Airbnb nearby, she packed up her stuff and I drove her and dropped her off thinking I would never, hopefully hear from her again.

No such luck. A few days later I got a message from her stating that she needed a few more days at the place. I told her no. And then she said, "I Facebook stalked your ex-wife and kids. What do you think they would say about what you did to me? And the pics I sent you and your responses…."

Extortion, this was new for me and I initially panicked. I had done a good job I thought of keeping my personal life secret and I didn't want my kids finding out so I gave in. I told her two more nights but no more. I contacted a lawyer friend about the situation and he said I should tell her that I would sue her if she continued the extortion. So, when as expected she texted again for more money, I told her no, threatened to sue her, blocked her, and never heard from her again.

The experience made me realize to be a bit more careful in my vetting process and a bit less generous in what I should offer without knowing what I was getting into. Unfortunately, that common sense was short lived and even more trouble was to come.

7) Strip clubs-

The night after Laura left, I felt like I needed to reboot. What better place than a strip club. I had never been to one (actually not true, I did go to one when I was about 25 at a friend's bachelor party but don't remember much about the experience). Of course, where I was psychologically at the time if I was going to do it, I was going to go all in. I turned to google maps to find the nearest club to me with the best reviews. I chose the Porthole Pub primarily due to proximity but also because the dancers were mostly black which I was beginning to realize was my preference in women.

Pulling into the rundown strip mall in which it was located I felt like I was coming home. I was even more comfortable as I walked into the bar with its thumping music, half-naked women, and the underlying vibe of depravity and sin. A place where anything could happen for a price. Just my type of place.

"What would you like?" the bartender asked while drying a glass.

"Vodka and tonic," I replied and then turned around to face the stage which was directly behind me. And there she was. The most beautiful woman I had ever seen. Of course, at this point I fell in love with every beautiful, sexually open woman that I met. Even just passing one on the street. I had an intimacy disorder, but I also had a love addiction. And it was fun!

Her eyes were outlined in shiny baby blue which matched her sequined tube top and too short skirt. As she flipped and squirmed on the pole, I watched the dynamic as men (and the occasional woman) moved up to the seats ringing the stage and waited for the young woman to slide, sway, or even tumble towards them. There she would seduce with her eyes, breasts, pelvis, legs, hands, even allowing some touching, but not too much. Then they would slide dollars into any band of clothing until she looked like a type of bird with feathers of dollars floating and flapping everywhere. Occasionally, someone would walk confidently up to stage, invite the woman over, and then toss a stack of money, drifting over her usually prone, outstretched form.

I asked for one-dollar bills from the bartender and headed up to the stage and waited. It didn't take long for her to pop up from a squat position where she had been nestling a man's head between her boobs and our eyes locked and we connected instantly. At least that was my alcohol lubricated interpretation.

"Hi handsome," she purred as she slowly crawled on all fours over to me and slipped her toned ebony arms around my neck.

"Hi," I replied, lost in her eyes. Black pupils blended with black irises into an open yet impenetrable disc of darkness. I knew I was in trouble.

"Haven't seen you here before," she said loud enough just to be heard over the throbbing bass.

"First time," I replied.

She pulled me closer and whispered in my ear, "Look forward to getting to know you better," and with that she sprung up and flung herself around the pole, twirling higher and higher until she was almost up against the ceiling, and then suddenly, plunged, stopping just inches from the stage. I was mesmerized by the combination of beauty, strength, coordination, sensuality, and sex, all obviously lubricated by alcohol.

I waited patiently until she finished her routine and then made eye contact with her as she left the stage, slipped between the red velvet chairs and small round tables, and headed towards me.

"Can I sit?" she asked and without waiting for an answer dropped her purse on the table and slid onto one of the seats next to me. She then pulled closer and placed her leg over mine and her arm around my neck.

Just then one of the waitresses stopped at our table. "Drinks?" she asked.

"Vodka tonic for me…." And I waited. "Patron shot, a double, with a side of 7 up."

"So," she said looking back to me, "I'm Ginger."

"Scott," I replied.

"So Scott," she whispered in my ear. "Would you like a dance?"

"Can you explain?" I asked. "I'm new to this."

Ginger laughed gently, covering her mouth with her hand.

"We go to the back for some private time," she started, already picking up her purse, "and you tip me 20 dollars for each song," by this time she was standing and holding out her hand to me.

"Sure," I stammered still unsure what to expect.

We headed past a few large men squeezed into too small red shirts with black vests to a row of curtained stalls and Ginger pulled back one and there was woman with her dress pulled up riding a guy in a sitting position.

"Whoops," Ginger said. "Sorry honey." And she moved to the next stall and gently pushed me down onto the stained and cracked dark brown vinyl banquette.

So, I quickly learned that in Florida strip clubs anything goes. For a price. Blowjobs for 30-100, sex for 200-400.

Afterwards, Ginger sat with me as we watched an obese woman in a too small outfit lounge naked on the stage.

"Can I get your number?" I asked.

"Sure," she purred and grabbed my phone and punched in the numbers.

The rest of the night passed as I learned they usually do in the clubs. Spending time with your regular girl, giving her 20-dollar tips periodically for sitting or going back with her and paying for dances, flirting and maybe even getting a dance with another girl while yours was on stage. Ginger quickly taught me how things worked and I appreciated how honest and upfront she was about what she does, why she does it, and what she imagined for her future. And by the time I left at 2 AM, about 1000 dollars poorer, I was addicted to yet another part of the world of sex.

8) SUGAR BABIES-

Ginger and I quickly fell into a routine. She would come over every few days, I would pay her 500 dollars, we would have sex (crazy, mad, passionate, fun sex), and then we would lie around naked for a while talking and then go out to dinner, a show, or a club. I met her dog, slept at her place, dropped her off at a music audition, brought her pizza while she was working at the club. She left home when she was 16 and basically had no relationship with her family (which she didn't want to get into), was mildly bipolar, drank a lot, didn't know how to cook, had a stripper pole in her apartment, and didn't like vegetables. She felt like a girlfriend who I paid. Which honestly wasn't much different that my marriage. Essentially my wife didn't work so I was basically paying for everything, and in exchange I got companionship and, up until the end, occasional sex. Although everything with Ginger was just so much more: more intense, more beautiful, more sensual/sexual, and more dangerous.

While I liked Ginger, being a good addict, I wanted even more. I was bored for the few days between our visits so I decided to branch out. I started to research other sites. I started spending a lot of time on What's Your Price. It's a site where you bid on dates with women.

I quickly learned that most women on the site were looking for some type of arrangement.

Either pay per meet (which is essentially what I had been doing with Ginger) with amounts ranging from 100-200 dollars for just dinner to 300-500 dollars for a date which included sex. At least this is what I figured out over time. The first woman I met on the site was Janice.

I'll be honest, one of the things I liked about Janice was she was cheaper than Ginger. Only 250 for a meet and I could even just get a blow job in the car for 60. But beyond that she was, similar to Ginger, short, black, had a beautiful body, no relationship with her family, was mildly bipolar, and drank a lot (and smoked a lot of weed). Unlike Ginger, she didn't dance. She said she was too shy. Instead to make money she worked at a massage parlor in a nearby strip mall. I'm sure you've seen them before and maybe already know what goes on in them.

For fun one night, I visited her at her work place but we agreed to pretend not to know each other. She was feeling that the other girls looked down on her for being black. Most of them were Cuban or Russian (nationalities which seemed the most common in the sex industry in South Florida). She wanted me to come in and choose her to raise her street cred. At that point I was down for anything so that night I went in and looked the other girls up and down and then chose Janice. The other girls sulked away into the back and Janice and I went into her massage room (after I paid the 200 for a "special" massage to the front desk manager, a big, ugly, musclebound Russian).

"So, what do you do normally?" I asked.

"Take off your clothes," she commanded.

I did as I was told and she placed a towel over my butt and then began massaging, starting from my back and moving down.

I soon learned, really the only difference between this and a normal massage was the "happy ending" which usually consisted of a hand job, or sometimes, a blow job, depending on the amount paid and the connection between the worker and client.

That night, while driving home, I had my first brush with the law. I had been drinking Prosecco at a local bar before heading to meet Ginger. I hadn't finished the bottle so grabbed it and placed it in my center console, cradled amongst my miscellaneous crap, but with the neck pointing conspicuously forward.

Honestly, I was pretty drunk, and definitely shouldn't have been driving but at that point in my life honestly, I was of the mind that up to now I hadn't been caught and would deal with it somehow if I was.

One thing I hadn't factored in was white privilege and the other intangibles that make a police officer target one person over another. I guess it's called profiling and I profile well. I'm a tall, white, well-dressed man. Unfair I know, but it's the system, especially in the section of South Florida I was in, which was essentially, what one could call, the "hood".

I was racing down Federal Highway, going about 80 in a 40 zone, drinking out of the bottle, and I didn't really see the lights behind me until I heard a gruff amplified voice say, "Pull over."

The weird thing was at that point in my life I didn't worry. I didn't even move the bottle out of the console. So, when the officer came over and looked into my car with his flashlight I, in retrospect, have no idea how he didn't see it.

"Do you know why I pulled you over?" he asked.

"I know officer," I said, trying to sound as sober as possible. "I was going a bit fast. I just have a family emergency at home that I'm trying to get to." And then I waited. I knew it was a lame excuse but preplanning at that point in life was not a strength.

And then amazingly the officer said, "Well just slow down and I hope all works out."

That was it. I waited for the officer to drive off and then I sped off myself, obviously not having learned an obvious lesson which would come back to haunt me later.

9) BB REDUX (AGAIN)
AND MY FIRST TATTOO-

I had lost touch with BB since the Bermuda debacle and so was mildly surprised when I received an email from her asking for me to fund her jail commissary account for $50 so she could email and text. Not knowing much about the jail communication system and always up for a new experience I said sure.

The next day I received a link the State of Georgia corrections website which instructed me how to send the money to BB's account. It was all fairly organized for what I thought would be a dysfunctional system. And the day after that I received my first secure email through the site from BB. Apparently, she had been in a bad car accident on the highway and due to her having a couple outstanding warrants on drug possession charges (and arguing with the police officer on the scene, she admitted) she had ended up in jail. She was mostly upset because her little dog Layla (a pug/terrier mix) had been in the passenger seat in kennel and had been flung out the door and slid 50 feet down the highway before skidding into the cement barrier in the center of the highway. Layla hadn't stopped shaking since the incident and that was BB's biggest concern. She had been there for a month waiting for sentencing and spent the first week in solitary, tied up to a chair, naked, and fed only when the guards would throw food onto the cement floor which she had to eat off the floor like a dog. She also didn't have a lawyer and didn't have a clue about when she was going to be released. So, I contacted her mom (who was taking care of Layla) and offered some money to help her get a lawyer. I know BB's mom loved her. I think at this point she was just sick of her life, the consequences, and was trying to give her some tough love.

"You do what you want," she said in a raspy voice, cigarette infused voice.

"Thanks," I replied.

She coughed and then added, "but just be careful. You know her some and you know it's just going to be more of the same."

"I know," I said, "but she's so lovable.

"I know," her mom replied and then I heard the phone click off.

A week later BB was released and wanted to come to visit me in Florida as a "thank you." I, of course, said sure, and that's how I found myself waiting at the Ft. Lauderdale airport, and waiting, and waiting.

A text. "Sorry babe. Missed my flight. Will be there tomorrow at 10. Love ya."

That was it. So hard not to love.

So back to my apartment and back to the airport in the morning.

Still no BB. Another text. "Sorry babe. I got stopped for having weed in my suitcase. And then I yelled at them and they banned me from Delta. I can get an American flight at 4."

In retrospect, it's odd that it all seemed so normal, but it did. So, I sat in the airport and waited. Plane lands at 4. Waiting. 5 o'clock and here comes BB down the stairs pulling an oversized carry on and the kennel with Layla barking loudly.

"Babe," she shouted, putting down her stuff and jumped up into my arms, startling the few remaining people at the baggage claim. She was high as fuck. I tried to follow her ramblings but I ended up just listening mostly while she discussed the experience at the airport, Layla's well-being, her relationship with her mother, and then she lit a cigarette, which of course, resulted in a uniformed airport staff member running over to us.

"Ma'am", she shouted. "You have to put that out. Now!"

"Wow!" BB shouted back. "You don't know what I've been dealing with. I just need a couple puffs." She said continuing to pull on the cigarette.

Just then two cops started coming towards us from down at the end of the hall.

"Scott," BB said to me. "There's my suitcase."

"BB," I said. "You go outside and put out the cigarette and I will get your bag."

"Bitch," BB said to the woman, picked up Layla's kennel, and walked to the sliding doors, and turned just to give the finger to the woman as the doors closed behind her.

The woman turned to me with a questioning and accusatory look. I just shrugged, grabbed BB's bags and wheeled them out to the curb where she was standing smoking away.

"Well, you're never boring," I said, stopping next to her.

"I missed you," BB said and jumped onto me again, almost knocking me into the oncoming traffic. "Let's get a tattoo," she added.

"A tattoo?" I asked, working hard to track the conversation and also remember where I parked.

"Yea!" she exclaimed. I want get an apple on my shoulder. "But a Gala apple. That's the only kind that I like as you know."

I did know that as I was instructed that the only things she wanted me to get for her visit were Gala apples and milk.

"Sure," I replied, giving into the BB experience.

"I know a place nearby," she said as I popped open the hatch of my silver Kia Soul and lugged her bags into the back. She slipped Layla out of her kennel and by the time I sat in the driver's seat BB was snoring gently and Layla was looking knowingly at me.

"Hey babe," I nudged her. "Give me the name of the place."

"Which place?" she purred, half asleep, or passed out.

"The tattoo place," I said patiently.

"Black Dog," she said and was out again.

I popped the name into my phone and 20 minutes later we were there. And two hours later I had a small Gala apple on my left wrist and BB had a large one on her left shoulder. Not much to say about the experience other than the tattoo artist recognized BB so I think did an extra special job on her.

My first (but not my last) matching tattoo completed, we headed to my oceanfront condo.

"Babe," BB said, after the tattoo was done, "can we make a quick stop on the way to your place?"

"Of course," I replied. And she typed in an address and off we went with Layla staring patiently through the front window.

Fifteen minutes later we pulled into a run-down strip mall.

"Go around back," she ordered while pointing down a dark and puddled driveway.

I turned and stopped next to two broken down pickups.

"I'll be right back," she said as she jumped out of the car and entered the back of the building.

I guess these are the times in retrospect I should have assessed my choices, my situation, my future. But instead, I reached into the backseat and popped open a Mikes harder lemonade, cranked up some reggaeton, and before I could even finish my drink she was back at the car.

"Mission accomplished," she said.

And we headed off to my apartment.

Most of the next few days was amazing. We ate at great restaurants, hit the local strip clubs, even went to a few museums. I loved being with BB. She was so fun and open to everything. And I loved the looks we got, especially from those who recognized her. I guess porn stars can be pretty famous these days. We were getting along really well. BB even asked me to go the "Porn star awards" in Las Vegas the next month as her date. She had been nominated for "Best anal" and was excited. I even drove her to one of her "dates" and waited at the restaurant of the hotel downstairs while she made 3000 dollars by allowing a man to spend two hours with her. She told me about 75% of the time she didn't even have sex with them. I guess they were under too much pressure to perform. While everything was good overall, BBs drug use was out of control. Her thing now was fentanyl. A lot of it. For those who don't know fentanyl is a super powerful opiate that has become very popular over the last few years. In addition, it's responsible for significant number of the overdoses during the "opiate epidemic" as it has a narrow window for effect and is being cut into other drugs without the user knowing.

One day I walked into my living room and she was crushing tabs and snorting them on my coffee table.

"Um," I said watching as she placed the leftovers inside her lower lip tattooed with "Bad Bitch".

"What?" she asked.

"Nothing," I said. But an hour later BB was almost incoherent. We were supposed to be going out to dinner but when I walked into the bathroom she was passed out, naked, her head in the sink, and a smear of red lipstick crossing her cheek.

"Guess we're not going out tonight," I said to myself and carried her into bed, tucking her under the comforter.

When I went back in the bathroom, there was a bottle of pills sitting there on the toilet.

I picked them up and looked at them. "Oxycontin" it said on the label. BB had told me that fentanyl was now being pressed into tablets and labeled as oxycontin so if one was stopped by the cops, they could say they had a prescription for it from their doctor.

I was drunk. I picked up the bottle and flushed them all down the toilet. Obviously wasn't thinking clearly

41

about how BB would react or how her body would deal with suddenly being cut off. I took the pill bottle and threw it over the balcony toward the ocean. And then I passed out only to be awakened what I guessed was a few hours later but things being thrown in the bathroom.

I got up and walked in and found BB on the floor frantically going through her toiletry bag.

"Scott?" she asked looking up at me with smudges of makeup tracking down her cheeks. "Have you seen my medicine?"

"No, sorry," I replied.

One thing about BB was she could smell a lie from a mile away. She launched at me and started screaming and punching me like a wild animal.

"I was going to sell that! It was a thousand dollars worth of stuff!" She screamed as she ran to the kitchen and started to go through the cabinets. "Where did you fucking put it!" she shouted. "Tell me goddamnit!" And then she started to take plates and fling them across the room at me, one of them denting the wall above my head before shattering. I tried to make my way to her while dodging the flying dishes. When I finally got to her, I tried to give her a hug to comfort her but also to stop the barrage.

"Get your fucking hands off of me!" she yelled. "I'm out of here!" she continued as she broke away and started to throw her clothes that were scattered around the apartment into her suitcase.

"Come on BB," I tried to calm her. "We can figure it out."

"You grabbed me!" she yelled. "You know what's happened to me."

"I was just trying to comfort you," I replied but I could tell by the look in her eyes that I had lost her, at least for now.

She put Layla in her kennel and struggled to the door with her belongings, opened the door and left, slamming the door behind her.

I waited a few minutes and headed downstairs to the lobby, and then headed out into the early morning darkness. I walked the streets for about an hour trying to find her. But she was gone.

10) Drugs-

Now with BB gone (again) I settled into a routine with Ginger and Janice (adding another girl I met on What's Your Price named Evelyn, Eve for short). I maintained a pay per meet deal with Ginger but moved to a monthly allowance arrangement with Janice and soon after with Eve. I gifted Ginger 1000 a month which included 4-5 "dates" a month and regular texting. Eve was 1500 as she was prettier and more kinky. She was really into collars/leashes, submission, and the "daddy" thing and it was different and fun.

However, after a couple months of the rotation I again got bored. Addiction is not rocket science. In retrospect I realized I was needing more and more to get the same dopamine hit in my brain. Any addiction would suffice be it women or alcohol or whatever new thing I hadn't yet tried.

So, I guess it comes as no surprise that I started to escalate in risk level regardless of the vice. Enter Jasmine (by now I'm sure you've realized that many of these women weren't using their real names. Sometimes it was their stripper/sex worker name, other times just a name they made up, rarely it was in fact their real name. Who knew? Reality was becoming less and less relevant. I had no job, lived on the beach, across from a bar, had money, and no one to keep me anchored so…

I met Jasmine on one of the escort sites which I still patrolled periodically. In retrospect, it was should have been a warning that she was only asking for 100 for sex but her picture was beautiful and her body checked my boxes: black, short, thin. There had to be a catch and I was curious. I headed over one afternoon, after a quick stop at the ATM, to a low rent, run down, strip mall motel off of Federal Highway in Fort Lauderdale. I even brought my pit bull/chihuahua mix with me, not sure why. I was already about 4 beers in so my decision making was just south of ok and I had another six pack in the back seat next to the dog.

I pulled into the parking lot between an old pick up filled with tires and a large barbeque smoker which was belching smoke and grabbed the beer and my dog and headed to Room 6. The route skirted the swimming pool which was filled with a group of Chinese kids smoking and drinking beers and an obese Russian couple sitting on the pool edge making out.

Finding the room, I knocked on the door. The window was covered with a sheet and the door was covered with a large brown stain that had bubbled the brown laminate so my knock put a hole in it and made almost no sound.

"Hello," I said, placing my mouth near the door.

Who would answer: a cop, a group of guys wanting to rob me, or the woman in the ad. Who knew? My dog was not super excited about the situation and was sitting next to me staring up with a concerned look.

Then the door opened and she was there. Just like her picture, other than her small toned body was covered with a sheet and she was busily shifting the dreadlocked wig on her head. The first thing that I noticed was she never stopped moving or talking or both. She was like an energizer bunny.

"Hi," she said hurriedly while quickly heading to the bed where she started to take off the sheet and pillowcases and put on new ones that were piled on the chair next to the bed. The room was dark and depressing and my dog was not impressed and continued to stare at me.

"Do you mind if I smoke?" she asked while continuing to race around the room.

"Not at all," I replied.

The pillowcases were only half-way on, the sheet was not large enough to completely cover the stained mattress, but at that point she sat on the edge of the bed.

"Do you smoke?" she asked.

"Sure," I replied assuming she meant weed which most women I knew at this point smoked.

Then she picked up a coke can and began an elaborate ritual of smoking a cigarette and taking the ashes and putting them on an indented side of the can. She then dropped a small white crystal into the ashes and while holding the improvised pipe with one hand, used the other one to light the mixture and then sucked through what appeared to be a hole that she had made in the side.

"Is that crack?" I asked.

"Yes," she laughed after blowing out the smoke. "Want a hit?"

I looked at my dog who was continuing to stare at me with the same look although now, impossibly, she looked more concerned than before.

"Sure," I replied, looking quickly back at Jasmine.

I remembered at that point an article I had read back in the 80s at the beginning of the crack epidemic about journalist who was writing an article about the drug. The story was that after one hit, he became addicted and ended up losing his job and family, winding up in jail. So, with that thought lingering, I took my first hit of crack. And I waited. And waited. After about 15 minutes all I can say I was underwhelmed. Maybe my dopamine receptors were already too saturated, but I didn't feel much. Just felt better than I had, more energy, more sensory, but that was about it.

However, the drug seemed to really change Janice. She went into overdrive almost immediately after her hit. She almost tore off my clothes and we had the craziest wild sex I had ever had and then after about an hour we collapsed, exhausted, into each other's arms and laid on the bed. I watched the old white metal ceiling fan, with wires hanging out of the base, wobbly rotate around and around.

We talked for a bit. I learned she was from Haiti and had come to the country illegally a couple years before. She had tried a few jobs but couldn't keep them due to a mental illness diagnosis which she didn't share, and had settled in with escorting. She would stay in one of these low budget motels for a week or so, until she was kicked out by management (who usually would look away for a while, but didn't want too much police attention). It was enough to pay for her meds which she bought off the street since she couldn't afford to see a psychiatrist and apparently enough to support her crack habit. Every hour while we talked, she fired up her homemade pipe and smoked and then we would have sex again. This cycle continued until my dog barked at the door and in walked a huge man dressed in a white t-shirt and baggy jeans with large gold chains hanging over his chest. He didn't even look at me as he took money from Janice and he dropped 5 more small rocks in her hand and then turned and walked back out the door. That was odd, I thought to myself. But at this point I don't know whether it was the beers, the crack, or the combination, but I wasn't one hundred percent sure what was real and what wasn't.

And that's pretty much how the next week went. I gave her about 200 dollars a day, and we would have sex, smoke, order out for pizza, take the dog for a walk, and repeat over and over again. It was drug and alcohol fueled, and it was fun! Until at some point something changed in Janice. She started to get paranoid that there was someone at the door, which was odd given she seemed to have no issue with the dealer coming into our room 4-5 times a day without knocking. Also, her mood started to change, while she had been energetic before, now her speech became pressured to the point of not being able complete her sentences. She would periodically start yelling at me for some perceived injustice: white privilege, misogyny, social injustice, racism. It got to the point where I suggested she go the hospital. We had been lying in bed sharing the last rock in the pile when she threw the can against the wall.

"Get the fuck out you racist, white, misogynistic whore!"

And she bounced off the bed, grabbed my clothes, went to the door, and threw them, then she stood there, completely naked, and just pointed with her eyes closed and her body twitching.

I took that as my cue and quickly picked up my dog and ran out of the room, picked up my clothes (which I put on while running), past the pool where the same groups lingered, not even glancing at the half naked white guy and his dog running across the lawn and out the gate.

11) The first bottom (Too many babies)-

I had a dysfunctional rhythm to my days now. Start drinking prosecco and orange juice when I woke up about noon, head out to happy hour at the bar across the street at 4, then pick up my dog and walk over to the small area of bars and restaurants a couple blocks from my place and basically drink and hang out until I passed out about midnight. There, of course, were deviations from the pattern. I still was seeing Ginger, Janice, and Eve regularly and heading to the strip club about once a week.

One afternoon, coming back from the happy hour bar I saw a beautiful blond woman walking barefoot down the street as I was driving home from the bars. That wasn't too weird, given it was South Florida. What was strange was that she was wearing only jeans. No top. And she was dancing down the side walk to a song only she could hear.

I pulled up alongside of her. "Are you ok?"

She didn't respond, so I stopped my car and got out. After having to shout to finally get her attention, she looked at me like she had just exited a trance. Her eyes cleared. They were crystal green like the shallows of the Caribbean Sea. Her body was tanned with no lines, and she had long blond hair which fell in tangled braids over her shoulders.

"Hi," she replied.

"Here," I said, slipping off my t-shirt and handing it to her. She looked at it and then slid it over her head and then stared at me.

"Thanks," she said, "I don't know where my clothes and shoes are," she adding, looking around. "Where am I?"

I was getting the idea, even in my inebriated state, that she was on something.

"You're near Oakland Park Boulevard," I said, "The ocean is over there," and I pointed behind us.

"Oh," she sighed.

"Do you need me to drive you somewhere?" I asked.

"Yes, please," she said quietly and put her hands in her jeans' pockets.

"Let's stop at my place to get me a shirt, ok?" I asked. "It's right here," I added, gesturing toward a large building on the next block.

"Sure," she said and got into my car.

We parked in my garage and passed the glaring front desk manager, who, after the BB debacle and the escorts and young women who frequented my apartment, was not my fan.

I waved at him anyway.

Once we entered my place, I went to the bedroom to get a shirt, and she followed closely behind.

"Can I give you a blowjob for helping me out?" she asked while putting on the t-shirt I had pulled out of the closet.

I thought about it, and I can say it was one of the few times during my run that I made a good choice. She looked like she was on fentanyl or meth and along with that was the risk she was shooting. I didn't want to get HIV, Hepatitis B or C, or both, so I declined.

She didn't say anything, and we headed out of the apartment and back down to the car.

"Where to?" I asked.

"Here's the address of where I'm staying," she said and handed me her phone.

We made small talk while driving the short distance. I stopped by the atm and gave her 200 dollars as she looked like she needed it. In retrospect, she probably used it for drugs but I felt sorry for her for some reason. She was so lovely, polite, and appreciative.

We pulled up in front of boarded up house, with the sounds of barking dogs and people yelling emanating from inside.

"You sure?" I asked.

"Yes," she said. Then she grabbed my phone, typed in her number, and slipped silently out of the car.

I watched as she entered the house, and then drove away, and despite messaging her a few times, never heard from her again.

A couple days later I headed off to the strip club to meet up with Franny, a new woman I had met on What's Your Price a few days before. She was tall, half Egyptian and half Puerto Rican, she told me during our chats. She had classically beautiful features and was wearing a bizarre range of outfits in her pictures ranging from a floral print dress to a killer short plaid skirt and long white stockings with black heels.

I had been waiting at the club for a few minutes when she pulled up in an Uber and stumbled out of the back door. She was drunk. Like really drunk. While I was past tipsy, I realized I would need to catch up. Nothing worse than being on different drunk levels with a date.

"Hey baby," she slurred while jumping into my arms.

"Hey," I replied, exiting the embrace. "Let's go," I said and we entered the club.

We were at Top Gun, definitely a step up from the Porthole. The dancers were a mix of Russian and Cuban, the bartenders were hot, and the drinks were very, very strong. The goal at a club is to get the patrons as drunk as possible so they would tip better. Despite knowing this I ordered a double vodka tonic.

"Cheers," I said and drained the cup.

It only took about a half hour to get to her level. And then the fun began. She stripped off her top to reveal a short crop top to go with her too short dress and she sat on my lap and started to grind methodically. I ran my hands along her back and around her ass.

"Go lower," she purred into my ear.

I realized then that she had no underwear on, and I slid my finger around her pussy.

"Grab my neck," she ordered.

I did what was told and she moaned as I choked her and then she grabbed my crotch and began rubbing gently.

"Slap me," she said and stared at me with almond brown eyes.

Just then, a bouncer, came up to us.

"You guys have to take this out of the club," he said and waited.

"We're just having a little fun," Franny said softly and tried to put her arm around him.

"Let's go," he said and grabbed us each by an arm and led us out the door to the parking lot.

"My place?" I asked.

"Sure," she replied and we headed to my car.

Once in the car she pulled up her skirt and grabbed my hand and slid my finger inside of her. "Drive," she said, and I did as ordered.

I was obviously way too drunk to drive and I had even more trouble trying to focus while she rode my fingers to an orgasm and then unzipped my jeans and started to give me a blow job while driving.

"Slap me on the ass," she said, lifting her head up briefly.

I knew there were women who liked things rough, so I went ahead and spanked her. When I did, she moaned loudly.

After I was done, she looked at me. And then out of the blue, with calm eyes, she punched me in the face. Not a gently punch but a full-on roundhouse. I swerved the car onto the side of the deserted road and stopped sideways on the shoulder.

"What the fuck!" I yelled.

She was laughing crazily. "You're bleeding!" she continued.

I looked in the mirror and I had blood streaming over my forehead and into my eyes. "You cut me with your ring!"

She continued to laugh.

"Get the fuck out!" I yelled and reached across her to open her door.

"Ok baby," she replied softly and got out of the car. I pulled back onto the road, the adrenaline for the time being making me feel sober. I grabbed an old t-shirt from my back seat and held it on my forehead and looked for a place to park to get a closer look at the damage.

I parked in a deserted taco bell parking lot and pulled back the t-shirt. I had a 3-inch cut running horizontally just below my hairline. The bleeding had slowed but there was still a slow ooze. Suddenly I felt sick and opened the door and threw up. That's the last thing I remember until the next morning when I woke up with blood all over my car, the door still open, and me still leaning out of the car with my head on the pavement. "I guess I passed out," I thought to myself.

The trip to the ER was a blur. In the waiting room I texted Franny to see how she was doing and to check whether she wanted to hang out again.

"I don't think we are healthy for each other," was all she said.

My next message went unanswered.

It took a few days for the nausea and headaches to ease up. I tried not drinking for a day but my body rebelled and I succumbed to the thirst but tempered the binging which had become my normal.

On the ride back from a daytime visit to the Porthole pub I stopped at a pizza place in a small strip mall near my apartment. In the parking lot there was a beautiful black woman with huge tits barely held in by her top, sitting on the curb next to a small purple suitcase.

Me, being such a good Samaritan, walked over to her.

"Are you ok?" I asked.

"No honey," she replied huskily, "I just got kicked out of my apartment and have nowhere to stay.

"Well, if you want you can stay at my place," I replied.

"That would be amazing sweetheart," she said.

"Let me get some pizza to go and I'll meet you by my car over there," I said, pointing to my silver Kia, still blood stained, but with no damage from the previous incident.

I could argue that my decision was poor due to a concussion or to blood loss but at that point I just couldn't process risk. I would do anything for pleasure.

So, with pizza box in hand, I headed to my car, dropped it in the back seat, grabbed her bag, put it in the hatch, and slipped into the driver's seat.

"What's your name?" I asked.

"Beth," she replied, while brushing mascara on her long lashes. She was a bigger woman, not my usual type, but her too short skirt and matching striped bra top were a turn on.

She had long black wig with the hair ends tied up in tangles of colored beads.

"Nice to meet you," I replied. "I'm Scott," and I reached out to shake her hand. Her grip was firm and her hand was large.

She went on to tell me about what had happened. Friends who told her she could live with them and then changed their minds after she moved in, a lost job, recent breakup, broken relationship with family.

After parking in my garage and another trip through the lobby (including the judging stare from the front desk manager) we entered my apartment.

"Drink?" I asked.

"Sure," she replied.

I opened up a bottle of Prosecco and brought the two glasses to the coffee table in front of the couch where Beth was sitting, puffing on a vape, and searching through her purse.

"All ok?" I asked after taking a sip.

"Yes," she replied. "I just can't find my wallet." She sighed and put the bag onto the table and picked up the glass. "Oh well. Just not my day I guess," and then she drained the glass.

By now I was sitting next to her on the couch next to her. I leaned over to her neck and started to kiss it. She leaned over, grabbed my crotch, until I started to harden. I pulled her top off revealing beautiful fake breasts, and after licking her nipples I began to make my way under her skirt when, Surprise!, she had a penis and balls.

"Oh," I said and pulled away.

"Sorry honey," he said. "Not what you expected?"

Now I had heard about this type of thing happening when I lived in Thailand. Some of the most beautiful women there were actually the so called "lady boys". But it was a new one for me.

Now I was a little stuck as I still thought she was beautiful and sexy but I just wasn't into dicks.

"How about a blow job?" I asked. Then added quickly, "For me."

To his credit he laughed. "Sure," and we headed to the bedroom.

The blowjob was incredible other than the moment I opened my eyes and saw that he was jerking himself off while deepthroating me. I closed my eyes quickly.

After I finished, he asked whether I wanted to fuck him in the ass. I declined and we got dressed and headed back to the couch where he went on to tell me about how he had always thought he was a woman since childhood and was waiting for the money to get the surgery. It was interesting to hear firsthand about his experiences and I ended up driving him a hotel room nearby for a few days.

"Thanks honey," he said, adjusting his dress and leaning over to give me a kiss on the cheek as he got out.

"Nice to meet you," I replied sincerely and drove out of the parking lot. Another box checked I guess, I thought to myself.

12) Geographical sobriety-

I was running out of money and realized I needed to get a job. I also knew that if I wanted to work, I had to get sober. Wasn't thrilled with the idea but they were the facts. I got a therapist, went to AA, and even joined an intensive outpatient program at a local rehab center. While I was able to stop drinking for a month or so (had to in order to stay in the outpatient rehab program), I couldn't stop seeing the women. I realized that I wasn't really being sober but it didn't really hit me that this plan wasn't working until my AA sponsor told me (after I showed him the newest matching tattoo, BEBE, I had gotten with Ginger, mine on the inner arm and hers below her belly button) that he would no longer sponsor me unless I stopped dating women, completely.

I was at a decision point and after some job searching, I found one in Kansas. I knew nothing about Kansas but figured it would be a place with fewer vices. South Florida I realized was not a place to be sober unless you were working a program which the addict in me refused to do. So, I tried what I later learned was called geographical sobriety. That by moving physically away from an addictive lifestyle somehow that will make you sober. Obviously, it's a ridiculous idea but at the time my addict brain was in charge and it would do anything to stay that way.

I toyed with the idea of moving Ginger, Janice and Eve out with me and maybe renting a 4-bedroom house in the country and doing the Charles Manson thing. All of them were open to it and Ginger even picked out a house. My sober brain was able to break through for a second and made me realize that it was not a good long term sober plan to be living in a house in the country with three sex workers who were all mentally unstable and had drug and alcohol issues. Little victories lol.

So, off I went (ignoring the "are you going to change your dog's name to Toto" and other Kansas jokes), packing up my Kia Soul with all my belongings (not much at the time), popping my dog in the passenger seat, and heading off on the 24-hour drive to my new home and sobriety.

I was completely committed to being sober from alcohol and women. It lasted three weeks. Like any good addict I restarted with drinking with conditions. Arriving during the summer, when the weather was nice, and living in the downtown area of the small Kansas City of Topeka, I would walk up to the few bar/brewpubs on the main street, sit with my dog outside, and have a couple beers. My deal with my therapist was I would only drink outside of the house, I wouldn't drink more than three beers a day, and I wouldn't drink hard alcohol. Obviously, once I started again, even with the clearly defined rules, it was just a matter of time before the rules would be broken. To be honest I don't remember what happened, but it did. Soon I found the downtown party crowd and the first thing to go was the daily limit. I figured that was ok as I was not drinking at home and was not drinking hard alcohol. And then, on my birthday in July, my friends bought me shots and what was I going to do? So, the only rule left was not drinking at home and that fell the next week. I don't remember the circumstances, probably because at that point it didn't take much.

It's funny (or maybe not) how easy it is for an addict to fail sobriety. And it was no different for the no women rule. That one fell in dramatic fashion.

I was relaxing with two of my friends, Bev and James, who at the time lived together in a loft above one of the downtown brewpubs. We were sitting on their back deck, looking out over the Capitol dome, drinking beers and listening to music when Bev got a call. She hung up and said, "We're going to a party," grabbed our hands, pulled us down the stairs, and out the door to the brewpub patio below.

Once there, a woman from a table of four shouted out to us and we headed over. Three I knew from past parties but one, a stunningly beautiful young blond, I didn't.

We pulled up some chairs. "This is Kala," one the girls introduced her to the rest of our group. We all said hi. I, however, was lost in Kala's light green eyes. They seemed to sparkle, reflecting the streetlights glare. The rest of her face and body were also perfect. I was in trouble again; I could feel it. As long as I didn't get too wasted, I told myself at the time, nothing will happen with her.

"There's a party over at the art gallery tonight," Bev added. "You guys want to join us?"

"Sure," Kala replied happily. Her energy was powerfully positive and I was already getting infected by her personality. "Definitely," the other three added. So, they paid their bill and we headed off to the Three Eagles art gallery which sat above The Iron Maiden (the only

Irish pub in town). The Three Eagles was one of the few art galleries in Topeka and its mission was to show and promote local artists. The owner, Ian, was a transplanted California hippie who had been attracted by the up-and-coming energy of the town and its low rents. We would spend evenings there checking out the art and listening to impromptu jam sessions on a small stage.

"Hey," Ian said as we came up the stairs.

After some pleasantries Ian asked, "Are you guys interested in going to a party in the tunnels tonight?"

"Tunnels?" I asked.

"There are some drainage tunnels that run under the city," he replied. "Occasionally we go down there and a few folks jam. The acoustics are incredible."

"Sure," we all replied at once.

"And this could add to the fun," he opened his hand and lying there on his palm were a lot of dried mushrooms. I hadn't done mushrooms since college when, not knowing what I was doing, ended up taking way too much and ended up on a paranoid mind trip with bleeding walls, morphing faces, and shifts of time and place which were terrifying. But, being a good addict, I took one from his palm and chewed it slowly. Tasted like dirt. The others followed my lead and then we headed back downstairs and to my car. I knew I was too drunk to drive, and I think everyone else was also.

"I'll drive," Kala said, and grabbed the key. The rest of looked at each other, shrugged, and jumped in. Kala's driving was terrible, and Ian at one point tried to open the car door while we were moving and jump out. Not sure if he was tripping but Bev grabbed him and pulled him back into the car.

I was definitely feeling the shrooms. Suddenly, everything felt possible, and everything was very, very funny. I was in the passenger seat and Kala reached over and put her hand on my leg. "How are you doing Scotty?" and she smiled coyly.

"I'm good," I smiled and looked over at her. Her face was glowing yellow and had a rim of orange surrounding her hair. I was staring at the light emanating from her head creating a halo that was getting larger and burning brighter, now a flaming red.

Ian broke the spell. "Stop here," he ordered and Kala pulled over to the side of the road.

Kala parked, partly on someone's lawn, and we piled out of the car, following Ian, wobbly, but following. He walked/slid down an embankment into a deep concrete drainage channel and then followed it until it entered a large cement tube, with darkness beyond.

The good and bad thing about being drunk and on drugs is that you do things that you would never do sober; unquestioning. Kala and I were holding hands and singing various theme songs from 1970's TV shows. We were half way through "Gilligan's Island" when we entered the tunnel. We stopped singing as we could hear some sort of music coming from deep in the darkness. Soon we entered a chamber, lit by candelabras lining the walls. Against one wall were two figures, dressed in black, one short and one tall, one playing a violin and one a cello. A soft sombre vibration filled the room. There were maybe twenty people positioned throughout, in different poses, seated cross-legged, standing in twos and threes, dancing with a slow writhing movement in the middle of the space.

Suddenly, somehow, I had a beer in my hand, and so did Kala, and so did the others in our group. Kala gripped my hand and led me to a distant wall. The beauty of sex on drugs and alcohol is there is no thought, no planning, no concern for the implications of the act. Primal pleasure. Of course, we were quiet, and tried to be as subtle as we could be given the circumstances. The reality was everyone was in their own world and completely unaware of what was going on in a darkened corner.

After, we headed back to Ian who was half-naked himself, dancing alone in the center of the room. We joined him, feeling the post-coital energy blending with the surreal atmosphere of the setting, and of course the drugs and alcohol.

A month into my stay in Kansas and geographical sobriety had officially failed.

13) KANSAS BABIES
AND MOLLY-

Kala left my apartment a couple of alcohol, drug, and sex fueled days later. The work week was starting and I had to get my shit together. My apartment was filled with beer and wine bottles from an impromptu party the night before and I spent Sunday afternoon cleaning up the mess and making the usual addict commitment that I would go back to doing this only on weekends, never during the work week.

Three days, six beers, and one strip club visit later, I was back to daily drinking.

I was honest with my therapist and she was supportive of my efforts, however limited. At this point the only sober thing I was doing was waking up, going to work, and holding off on drinking until I got home.

I was on Tinder and What's your price regularly and was pleasantly surprised that with the cheaper cost of living in the Midwest not only were milk and bread less expensive, but so were sugar babies. 100 for a date and 300 for a date with sex was standard. And off I went.

And of course, the strip clubs were a bargain also. I guess I should've known there would be strip clubs even in a place like Topeka. And The Baby Gallery was a good one by any standard. The women were beautiful, friendly, and I quickly became a regular, visiting at least twice a week. I would also usually spend 500 which I'm sure improved my popularity lol. But it also did seem that many of the women just wanted someone to talk to and listen to their issues regarding boyfriends, kids, jobs, housing, etc. I had a table which was a safe space for the women to come and not feel harassed. I had my favorites and soon was dating a couple of them outside of the club.

I also had expanded my chemical abuse to Molly. For those of you who don't know, Molly and Ecstasy are both slang terms for MDMA, a party drug that ravers prefer and also increases pleasurable feelings in general, no matter what you're doing.

My first experience with it was not great. I was on a date in Kansas City with a beautiful young black woman named Raven I had met on Tinder. This was the first unpaid Tinder date I had been on. She was bit older, 28 I think, and was a successful professional who just happened to like older guys. We went out to a jazz club and soon a younger blond came up to us while we were sitting at a small table in the corner.

"Sorry to bother you," she said shyly, twirling her long hair with her index finger. "Can I sit with you guys? You seem cool and my boyfriend and I had a fight and I just don't want to be alone."

This is interesting. I thought to myself and got up to pull another chair over to our table.

"I'm Beth," she said softly.

She was lovely. And in my alcohol fueled reality she looked almost angelic in a white dress and her hair pulled back with a band of yellow flowers.

"I'm Scott and this is Raven," I introduced us, and we sat back and listened to the jazz quartet for awhile without speaking. I enjoyed the energy of being surrounded by beauty, the two women, the setting, the music.

After the set ended, Beth reached into her pocket and handed us each a tablet.

"What is it?" I asked after swallowing it with a chug of beer.

"Molly," she said as she handed one to Raven who also downed it quickly.

"Cool," I said as I had always wanted to try it.

"Was supposed to be doing it with my boyfriend," she added, her voice trailing off.

"Well to new friends!" Raising my glass, the two women joined in the toast.

At that point I probably should have slowed my drinking down to see what kind of effect the drug was going to have on me, but… I didn't and as I got drunker and the Molly kicked in, everything became a swirl of beauty: the women (an arm around each one), the music (sultry and throbbing), and the soft yellow glow of the lights.

Around that time, reality became unhinged, and I just remember snippets in time: kissing Raven, holding hands with Beth, and then, weirdly, smelling Beth's hair; not a good sign.

"You guys interested in a threesome?" I asked at some point. "We could go to the hotel next door."

I guess I misread the room as the next thing I remember was sitting alone at the table and they both were gone. I got up and searched the club and the sidewalk outside. And then in the distance I saw what looked like the two of them, walking hand in hand down the street.

At that point I was rolling on the Molly (apparently that's the term) and too drunk to care so I stumbled over to my car. I was so awake (thanks Molly!) but I somehow knew I shouldn't drive, so I just sat in the car for an hour or so and then drove back to Topeka.

When I arrived back home, I wandered the apartment for hours, watched tik-tok videos, walked my dog, did the dishes, and swore I would never do Molly again.

14) First trip to jail-

So, I guess unsurprisingly, Raven and Beth didn't answer any of my texts that night or the next day so off I headed to the strip club to clear my head.

The moment I walked in I saw a dark haired, slim, heavily tattooed woman strut across the stage and then sling herself around the pole, over and over, until I was almost vertiginous.

She dropped to the floor and crawled over to me. She was high as fuck and her eyes could hardly focus.

"Let's dance when I'm done," she said into my ear, as she slipped her arms around my shoulders.

"Okay," I replied. Her sensuality was impossible to ignore.

I sat at the edge of the stage, and watched her in awe. She was so strong, so confident, so agile, despite being as drunk or drugged out as she was. It was an impressive feat.

After she finished, she sat next to me at the bar.

"Shots?" she asked.

"Sure," I replied. At that point I was fairly drunk and definitely drunk enough to have forgotten that shots are never a good idea.

"Tequila it is!" she smiled and ordered a couple from the bartender. Oh boy..

And that's how it began. Shots, dances in the back room, more shots, and still more shots. I couldn't believe she was still standing.

Then the lights came on. Literally. It was 2AM and the club was closing.

"Want to come over to my place?" she asked, smiling seductively.

"Sure," I replied. "Where do you live?"

"I'll text you my address," she said and then got up and walked back to the dressing room.

"Everybody out!" the bouncer announced and the patrons filed toward the exit.

I didn't feel very drunk, but about a mile in towards her place, it was as if the alcohol hit my brain all at once and I pulled over to the side of the road and passed out.

"Sir!" I heard the tapping softly at first but then it got louder and louder until it was like someone was banging on my head with a hammer.

Where was I? I thought to myself, and, What the hell is that noise?

I opened my eyes and with my head already turned towards the left I found myself staring directly into the face of one of Topeka's finest.

Shit!

I pressed the button and the window opened.

"Hello officer," I said as soberly as possible. I realized that obviously not enough time had passed to sober me up completely.

"License and registration," he demanded.

I fumbled around the glove box but couldn't find them.

"Please step out of the vehicle," he said while moving away from my car.

I pretty much knew at this point that I was fucked. Oh well, I thought and forced myself up and out the door.

"I can smell alcohol on you and your car is running so I'm going to give you a field sobriety test."

"Ok," I said. I was trying to sober myself up but I guess that's not actually possible as I could tell by his reaction to the nystagmus eye testing. And my performance walking a straight line heel to toe was not impressive. So…

"I'm going to take you down to the station for breath testing," he stated flatly.

At this point I had accepted my fate. I mean I had driven drunk my whole life and I guess this was my time.

"Ok," was all I could manage and he handcuffed me and stuffed me into the back of the cruiser.

The ride to the station was quiet, other than the occasional calls that squawked from his radio. I tried to make small talk but he wasn't interested.

Believe it or not I had never been in a police station before and it was just like the movies: the disinterested officer behind plexiglass at the front, the main office space with a few cops milling about; the air filled with bureaucracy and power.

"Sit there," my cop demanded, and I slid onto the stained light brown wooden chair as directed.

Without speaking he handed me a plastic tube attached to a small square white box and said, "Blow." And I did. I could see the number after, .160. I didn't know the exact cutoff but I knew that was too high.

"Come with me," he said while getting up and I followed him out of the office and down the hall to the main booking area, complete with a central control area and small cells behind.

So, I went through the process I had only seen on TV or in the movies. I handed over the contents of my pockets (including my driver's license), signed a bunch of paperwork, and tried to be as friendly to my new captors as possible. My efforts were not reciprocated, and I was soon in a small holding cell, complete with a concrete slab bench and walls smeared with various shades of browns, blacks, and reds. I passed the time trying to match the colors with bodily substances.

I was given the opportunity to make a call and I left a message on one of my friend's phones and then I waited. That was my take home from my first jail time. It's boring. At least I was still drunk so I didn't mind sleeping on the cold slab against the wall. The only annoyance was the guy in the cell next to me who kept screaming and ranting about the "system" and how he was friends with the governor and all the cops here were going to be fired when he got out to which the police periodically shouted, "Shut up Fred."

And that how the next 12 hours passed, until, after signing some more papers, getting another breath test (.06…), and receiving my phone, credit card, and a pink photocopy paper that was to act as my new license for the time being, I was released into the sun and into the waiting arms of three of my friends.

By that time, it was 4 PM, happy hour!

"Seriously?" my friends responded when I suggested heading to the bar.

"Of course," I replied, "What else am I supposed to do after my first jail stint."

So off we headed, then to the strip club with obviously no lessons learned from the experience.

15) LACEY
AND MORE DRUGS-

To compound my lack of changes in behavior, again the reality of being a privileged white male kicked in. I hired a good lawyer who was able to get me what's called a diversion, which essentially struck the DUI from my record. Score!

So back to what was now my routine. That was until I met Lacey.

Of all the women I had met, Lacey was the most extreme. She was the most beautiful, had the best body, was the most bipolar, used the greatest range of pharmaceuticals, was the most open to anything, and was just 21. A lot of rough life experience in not a lot of time also added to the experience.

And after our first Tinder date, which was essentially a pay for sex meet, our relationship became more complicated than a label. I would help her with her rent periodically (she was living with some other women in an apartment in a nearby college town while she was completing university), pay for our lunches and dinners, and cover the costs of the trips we went on. But after she flipped her car on the highway and rehabbed at my apartment, she spent more time at my place than hers. She labeled it 80 percent boyfriend/20 percent sugar daddy which seemed about right.

Our first trip was a drug fueled experience in NYC to meet an old rehab friend from the Meadows and show her New York. I had grown up there and was excited to share the experiences of the big city with her. She had been raised in a small Kansas town of 300 people and I was interested in what her impressions and experience would be.

So, I booked a 5-star hotel in downtown, made reservations at fine French restaurants, and planned excursions to musuems and Broadway shows. And off we went. Little did I know that addiction would destroy our first trip.

At first things went great, we went to Central Park, ate pizza with our hands, visited the Metropolitan Museum of Art, and had a wonderful late lunch with roasted duck and pan seared scallops.

And then we went to meet Jerome. He was a disbarred lawyer who had been my roommate at the Meadows rehab. While I failed out a week before leaving, I don't think Jerome had ever really tried sobriety, even in a rehab. It had apparently taken him a week to come down from the amount of cocaine he had been using and he had been to over 20 rehabs in his life. Luckily for him his mother was very wealthy and hadn't given up on him.

As a roommate, Jerome was great: funny, friendly, supportive, but I had never met him using..

So, Lacey and I headed over to his townhouse in a flashy part of Brooklyn.

"Dude!" he shouted when he opened the door, and enveloped me in a bear hug.

"This is Lacey," I said as he came over and gave her another hug.

"Great to meet you!" he exclaimed as he finally released her. Lacey's pale white cheeks were flushed.

In retrospect, the energy and enthusiasm Jerome demonstrated should have been a warning for what was to happen that evening.

The first sign things would be crazy was the behavior of Eileen, his gf, who literally ran across the room when we entered and jumped up on Lacey. It seemed just weird.

"OMG!" she shouted, "Come with me, what can we get you?" she asked while heading to the refrigerator, still clinging to Lacey's hand. She was non-stop motion and Lacey seemed a little overwhelmed. Jerome, meanwhile, was not much better, he had unending questions and observations, and I had trouble following his train of thought.

Then I saw the pipe on the coffee table. It was small and made of blue glass with some foil lining the bowl. It didn't look like it was for weed but I wasn't sure.

"Sit!" Eileen ordered us as she flung herself dramatically onto the sofa.

Eileen was Russian according to Jerome who had told me about her in rehab. Their relationship was rocky to say the least with her drugs of choice being bath salts, MDMA, and meth which were not a complement to her mostly manic bipolar disorder. This led to many police visits to the apartment, including the most recent where they both were arrested at the same time for domestic violence.

We did as we were told and were quickly offered some weed which all shared, then some lines of coke, which we all did, and then Jerome took some small packs out of his pocket and dropped the contents onto the aluminum foil on the end of the pipe.

"Want to try it?" he asked as he lit the top of the foil and took a hit.

"What is it? I asked.

"Meth," Eileen replied, as she took the pipe and did a hit.

By this point Lacey and I were feeling the effects of alcohol, weed, and coke and our inhibitions were falling quickly.

Something weird was happening with Jerome however. He was starting to get emotional and withdrawn. I tried to talk to him but he was shutting down.

"Let me talk to him," Lacey said and took his hand and led him to the bathroom.

I sat in the living room with Eileen and smoked more, drank more and talked about who knows what for who knows how long.

At some point Lacey and Jerome came out of the bathroom.

"What the fuck!" Eileen yelled. "You're such a slut! Jerome, your zipper is down!"

And before I knew what was happening, Eileen and Jerome were screaming and soon they started swinging at each other. Lacey was sitting on the couch, staring forward and I jumped off and tried to get between the two but soon Jerome was coming after me, swinging.

"Lacey, let's get out of here!" I shouted to her but she was still staring at the wall.

Eileen ran out of the apartment yelling about calling the cops.

"What the fuck is going on?" I asked.

"Nothing happened dude," Jerome said, running his hands through his hair.

"Ok," I said but the meth was making me really paranoid and I had trouble believing him especially given how strange Lacey was acting.

"I think we should leave," I said to Lacey.

"I want to stay," she said.

Just then the doorbell rang and in walked a group of 6 or 7 guys and girls dressed in various shades of black. They quickly made themselves at home and I realized this get together was a normal event.

Soon everyone was smoking meth. Lacey had returned from her daze and was quickly making new friends. I, on other hand, was getting more and more paranoid.

"I'm leaving," I said. "Find your own way back to Kansas." And I left the apartment and headed into the night air.

Outside my head cleared a bit and I realized I couldn't leave her there so I headed back and buzzed the bell.

Lacey showed up in the hallway.

"What the fuck!" she yelled. "You were going to leave me here."

Seeing her set me off again and I began punching walls and rushed to the apartment. I banged open the door and rushed at Jerome. Soon we were being pulled apart by the group.

Finally, things calmed down and the evening slowed a bit. We smoked in the closet and I think my mind went into some new place and before I knew it the morning light was drifting in the windows and it was just me, Lacey, and Jerome sitting on the couches making small talk.

"I gotta go crash," I said to them. "Did anything happen with you guys?" I had to ask as I got up and headed toward the door.

"Definitely not dude!" Jerome tried to be reassuring. "Eileen is so fucking paranoid!"

Lacey got up and followed me toward the door.

"Bye Jerome," she said, turning before leaving.

Outside the streets were busy with morning rush hour traffic.

I was starting to sober up and the realities of the evening were rushing back.

"Let's go back to Kansas," I said.

"Ok," Lacey replied emotionlessly.

And despite having two more days scheduled, I changed the plane tickets, and we went back to the hotel, packed, and flew back to Kansas without saying more than a few words to each other.

Back in Kansas I dropped her off at her place and then fell into a deep and dark depression. I hadn't completely realized how strongly I felt about Lacey but the idea that I still had doubts about what had happened between her and Jerome and that I didn't fully believe her, haunted me. I had read about this feeling but nothing prepared me for the next 7 days. I didn't eat, didn't sleep, didn't talk to anyone. I lost 15 pounds and mostly just stared at the wall.

I had finally found the person I imagined being with forever and then this happened. My inadequacies which I was treating with alcohol and younger women now flooded forward. I felt betrayed and hopeless.

16) Reality (and acid)-

With the fantasy of a life with Lacey upended I tried to settle back into a normal routine. Work, beers, bars, sometimes strip clubs, but I knew I couldn't give up on Lacey. Especially when there was still no clarity about what had actually happened. In her defense, she had been clear that we were not going to be monogamous, that she was just 21 and still wanted to experience more of life.

I realized I needed to accept the fact that if I wanted her in my life, I would have to allow her to continue to grow and experiment. So, I called her and soon we had fallen back into our old routine. She lived with me but I felt different. Like the bubble had burst. She was now more like how an alcoholic looks at beer, a necessary evil to keep the cravings at bay but not giving the satisfaction it had historically.

I learned to accept her online relationship with an an older European man and even some ongoing contact with Jerome. It was the cost to continue to have her in my life. Meanwhile, she continued to struggle with depression and drug use.

"Do you think you need more help?" I asked one morning while we were lying in bed watching the sun rise over the capitol building.

"Probably," she said, stretching, her naked pale body, tinted orange by the morning light filtering though the bedroom windows.

With that, we searched for a rehab that treated substance abuse, mental illness, and trauma. We finally found one and her admission date was scheduled in two weeks.

"Well, we might as well have some fun before I leave," she said playfully.

Acid.

I hadn't done it before but sometimes on a lot of mushrooms I would experience some hallucinations but nothing prepared me for our experience.

Thank god we picked a Friday night. We had no idea what we were doing and in retrospect our plan to do acid and go to the casino was unrealistic.

"Ready?" she asked taking two capsules out of a small vial.

"Sure," I replied and I placed one of them on my tongue while she placed the other on hers. And we waited.

Soon, while were talking, half of Lacey's face suddenly began to melt and started whirling into abstract shapes. "Whoa," I said. I assume she was experiencing something similar based on how she was staring at me.

I looked over at my dog who was looking at us uncertainly.

Then suddenly the floor below the couch was filling with water.

"Shit!" I said, jumping off it onto a throw pillow I had tossed into the now flowing river. Instead, it was now liquid shit, and I grabbed Lacey's hand, and we jumped from object to object, trying to avoid falling in.

I wasn't sure she saw what I did but she followed my lead as we skipped, carefully, down the hall into the bedroom where the floor was elevated above the streaming feces.

"Made it!" I exclaimed and lied down on the floor with Lacey and we stared at the ceiling. Gradually the textured cement began pulsating and the parts retracted, deeper and deeper into long black tunnels that led up into the sky.

"I don't think we should go the casino," Lacey laughed in a moment of clarity.

I smiled. "Probably not," still watching the show on the ceiling.

"Let's go for a walk," she said grabbing my hand and leading me back downstream, using the same objects we had used before to make it to the door.

Outside, there was a car parked in front of my apartment.

"Todd!" Lacey shouted and ran over, barefoot, to the car. I followed unsteadily, not sure what was real and what wasn't.

"This is a friend from college," she introduced me to the driver.

What was he doing here? Outside our apartment.

"Bye!" she shouted to him and grabbed my hand, and we ran up the street toward town.

Suddenly a police cruiser drove by and Lacey pulled up her top towards it, laughing hysterically.

I realized, in a moment of improved clarity, we needed to get back to the safety of the apartment. Steering her around, we headed back. The car in front was gone. Had it ever been there?

Upstairs, the river was gone. We sat on the couch. I watched the trees in a painting across from us grow and grow until the branches covered the wall. Then I turned back to Lacey. Her face started to age: she was 30, then 40, and kept changing until, in front of me there was a 90 year old version of Lacey: skin sagging and weathered but still with electric green eyes; and then she gradually got younger and younger until she was today's Lacey. And then she looked like me, a reflection, but me when I was 10, and I was being yelled at by a coach: "Do it again!" he yelled again and again.

And then I was in bed with Lacey somehow. She was freaking out. "I need it to stop! I need to go to the hospital". I looked at my watch. 8 hours had passed since we dosed. I don't know if I had slept but I was feeling like reality was returning.

I spent the next few hours reassuring her that it would end soon, and massaging her neck and back. And then we fell asleep.

A couple days later, we flew down to a condo I owned on the beach in Mexico. We had decided to spend her last free time before rehab in a new environment and after the acid trip, we were both ready to try some sobriety.

So, for the next two weeks, we led a normal life: cooked breakfast, meditated, did yoga, snorkeled on the reef outside the condo, made love, took photos, ate candlelit dinners on the beach, and slept. It was the first time I could remember (other than jail or rehab) being sober for that long. It was comfortable and I was happy, but in my heart, I knew it would all come crashing down when she left.

17) Jail (again)-

And it did.

I lasted until the night after I put her on a plane to rehab in Arizona before heading to the club. I fell back in with the same strippers I had spent time with before the months with Lacey.

Life was getting more dysfunctional. I was drinking more and later into the night and early morning. I was hungover and throwing up at work, frequently calling in sick. Every surface in my apartment was covered with beer and wine bottles. Once a week I would get a cart to transfer them all to the basement garbage bin. I would say I was done having realized when sober how much I had been drinking. I got an app to track my intake and, after hitting 100 drinks in a week, I deleted the app.

Escorts had never been a big part of my addiction but I needed a quick fix so I found them. Cheap ones in town, expensive ones in the city, porn stars visiting from out of town. I became a regular with a few of them.

I also got extorted by a woman who called my job and told them that I was drinking with underage women at the strip club. I guess I knew some of the dancers were under 21, but I didn't care at that point.

The months passed this way and in retrospect it was unsustainable, but I had no way of stopping. My friends enabled me, my kids didn't know how bad things were, my therapist tried to help, but I knew I had to make the decision to change.

In the end the decision, as expected, was made for me. Jail, rehab, hospital, or death. Those are the options in deep addiction. My recovery started with going back to jail.

Thanksgiving weekend.

Somehow, I still had maintained a relationship with my kids. They were in their late 20's. They knew I had continued to date younger women after the experience with BB and I was aware they didn't like it, but I wasn't going to stop for anyone at this point. They also knew that I was drinking too much and had suggested rehab a few times but thankfully didn't push it with me.

I was flying to NYC to see them. Drinking on the plane followed by, my favorite place, an airport bar, to spend some time before catching an uber to their neighborhood. I wasn't going to see them until the next day so I basically had the evening for myself before heading to see them. I sat at the bar drinking 20-dollar glasses of prosecco, and searching Tinder for someone who wanted to meet up. Airport bars are great for meeting people. A cross section of society, not tethered to their home, lubricated with alcohol.

Two hundred dollars of drinks later (in my defense I also bought drinks for many of the folks I met at the bar), I headed off to my Airbnb (my kids didn't want me to stay with them). Halfway there I realized I had left my laptop and suitcase at the bar. I really wasn't too surprised, at that point I was losing a credit card a month and had lost a jacket, gloves, hat, even left my dog at a bar once, only to have her running down the street to catch up with me.

I got to my place and passed out only to be woken at 6AM with the sound of trash trucks banging around containers right outside my window.

"Fuck," I said, feeling the hangover headache taking over quickly.

I got dressed and headed to a local coffee shop and spent the next few hours contacting the airport to see how to get in the arrival area to get my bag. They told me I could come to the lost and found to see if it had been dropped there.

The next couple days passed without incident. The time with my kids was nice (I tried not to be too drunk when seeing them) and it was helpful in a way to not spend the night at their place so I could drink and hook up with escorts in the evenings.

Miraculously my bag was found (minus 100 dollars in cash) and the next day I headed back to Kansas.

I kind of knew it was just a matter of time until something gave.

The trip home was more of the same: drinking on the flight, on the layover, on the flight, at the airport lounge, and it was only 2 pm when I landed. By that point my decision making was broken and I decided I should stop at a strip club off the highway on the way home to celebrate finding my bag. Any excuse. And then another club closer to home, then another. Until somehow, it was 2 AM and I was two blocks from home when I saw the flashing lights in my rearview mirror.

"Shit," I said aloud. I knew from my last experience that despite feeling sober I was not going to pass if I was tested.

"Hi officer," I said after rolling down my window.

"Step out of the car," he replied.

I tried to act sober as I opened the door and stood alongside the car.

Well, unsurprisingly I failed the field test again, and off I went back to Shawnee County jail. This time however, my phone was dead, and I didn't remember any of my friends' numbers, and the desk officers weren't amenable to me charging my phone behind their desk.

I was fucked.

So, I sat in the cell after processing. This time I was placed into a 6-person cell, three bunk beds, a metal toilet and sink in the corner. And I waited. Not sure what I was waiting for as no one obviously knew I was here.

I spent the next 4 days dealing with the drama of the lives of my cell mates: the schizophrenic who would rant all night nonsensically, the deaf older man who slept all day and ate everyone else's uneaten food, the young man who had hit someone driving drunk and was trying to deal with having to spend the next 7 years of his life in prison. I still had no idea how I was going to get out.

"Johnson," the guard said knocking on the cell door, "come with me."

I followed the guard to the desk and was told to wait for the bail bondsmen to come get me. I had no idea what was going on so I just sat and waited. A lot of that in jail.

After an hour or so, a middle-aged woman, fairly well dressed in a sweater and jeans walked up to the desk.

"Johnson," the guard said without looking up.

I headed up to the desk.

"I'm Alice," the woman said, sticking her hand out to me, "I'm your bailbondsman. Or woman." She laughed. "I'll sign you out and then we will head over to my office to get you fit with your ankle monitor."

"Ankle monitor?" I asked.

"Yes," she continued while signing papers, "the condition of your release was that you wear an alcohol ankle monitor for two months. It measures the alcohol in your sweat every hour and sends the data every 24 hours to me."

"Damn," I said aloud. "How did you know I was here?" I asked, while still processing the ankle monitor idea.

"Your colleague called me," she explained. "When you didn't show up to work, she was worried, and I guess she knew where to look." She looked at me and smiled sadly.

"Got it," I replied.

"Well, let's go," she said and we headed to the door and freedom. Sort of, as she wouldn't let me stop at the bar for a drink before getting the monitor...

18) Rehab (again)-

Within a few days of release from jail I was fired. I guess I wasn't surprised since my mugshot was all over the internet and my position required a morally clean public persona.

My lawyer who had been helpful (for about 10k) getting me a diversion for the first DUI and now for another 10k she said she could get me off on the driving without a license (no idea where it was), speeding, and reckless driving. For this DUI I would not have to do any more jail time, but I would have to pay a fine, have my license restricted to driving to work and treatment for one year, and get a breathalyzer installed in my car and use it for five years. Overall, not too bad I thought.

Sitting at home, unemployed, with my ankle monitor on (surprisingly not too uncomfortable and easy to hide under a sock) it finally hit me I needed to do something different. It wasn't a god moment but I realized what I was doing was unsustainable so I called around to rehabs. This time for alcohol.

After the Meadows, I had kept in touch with Sam, one of the others in my therapy group, who also lived in Florida. We had coffee regularly and he was supportive and sober until he relapsed and died in a hotel room from fentanyl-laced oxycodone with a Colombian prostitute, right before I moved to Kansas. After his death, I became friends and a support to his wife, Jane, who I had briefly met during a family weekend. She was a rehab counselor in south Florida, and I figured she would have advice about where to go.

"Hello," she answered when I called.

"Hey," I replied.

After the usual pleasantries, I explained to her what had happened and asked her opinion about where to go.

"Why don't you come to my place," she exclaimed. "It's called New Frontiers and it's in Ft. Lauderdale."

I had been thinking about staying in Kansas, but it was winter and the idea of spending the next 45 days or so in the sun and warmth while getting sober sounded appealing.

"I'll check into it," I said. "Thanks Jane."

After hanging up the phone I did some internet sleuthing on the program. It was only 30-days (so they said on the site) and there was no mention of 12 steps (lie). My insurance would cover the cost, so after dropping my dog off at my son's place, off I went.

Unfortunately, with the ankle monitor I couldn't do the usual drinking and drug spree most people do before arriving at rehab. So, I arrived at Ft Lauderdale airport stone cold sober and got picked up by a man who looked like a Hell's angel, tatted up, thinning hair pulled back in a ponytail, and wearing a denim vest.

He grabbed my bag and I followed him out of the airport into the Florida sunshine.

Southeast Florida is rehab central. The joke is that 50% of people are addicts and the other 50% are in recovery.

People make it sound like rehab is difficult. Other than the withdrawal, which depending on the drug of choice can range from none, to as long as 30 days for things like benzos, it's more like summer camp with a lot of group therapy. Freshly cooked meals, field trips to beach and park, movie nights, and best of all after insurance it was free!

The other inmates (as we called ourselves) were a diverse group: John the middle-aged alcoholic tennis pro, Desi the 20-year-old fentanyl addicted college student, Robert the elderly retired coke and meth addict, and on and on. We would sit in the courtyard between group sessions, smoking, sharing war stories of our battles with addiction. The most sobering thought for all of us was when we were told only three percent of us would be sober in a year. Who would it be?

The twelve steps of AA would apparently be our gospel. And along with AA comes God. They tell you that it can be a spirituality of your understanding, but the reality is, it's God. Not being raised in a religious house (more the opposite) it was tough to accept. However, I found that with daily prayer, and giving up the ego control that we addicts are so good at, things got better. At least the cravings for alcohol improved. The problem was Desi. She was just my type: drug addicted, bipolar, and had a terrible upbringing with abuse and neglect. My therapist, Todd, suggested I stay away from her as he, likely correctly, thought any relationship between the two of us would result in trauma bonding and would harm our recovery. True, but...

One theory is that addicts have low dopamine neurotransmitter levels and they use in order to get to the levels (and beyond) of "normal" people. And for many addicts, they will do whatever they have to in order to get that dopamine hit. Drugs, alcohol, gambling, sex, shopping, eating. Of course, addicts have their drug of choice, however, plenty of them will practice addiction substitution and gamble when they can't get coke for example. So, despite not having alcohol, I had Desi. And despite the staff's best efforts we managed to spend most evenings chatting deep into the night.

I know it's the elephant in the room so let's talk about it. I liked younger women. But only a certain type. I had no interest in the run of the mill 20-year-old. They were boring. But add drugs, mental illness, and trauma and they became interesting. Poetic, artistic, creative, looking at the world in a different way which was refreshing and honest. And of course, having had an emotionally neglectful upbringing, trauma bonding, the draw between people who have that shared experience, is powerful and ageless.

It was her fourth rehab and per her this would be her last. Her family was running out of money and patience. Of course, the irony is their emotional neglect led her to the streets and prostituting herself in order to pay for her habit. However, she was resilient, and despite the challenges, was able to somehow finish high school and her first year of college. Rehab over her winter break was the plan and then back to school. What a life.

"We should get tattoos when we get out," I said one night while we were sitting in the courtyard smoking cigarettes.

Desi put hers out and looked up at the stars. "Sure," she said quietly, "I want a smiley face." And she pulled out the drawing pad she carried with her and sketched out a yellow smiley face, a classic from the 1970s. It looked so innocent and pure. So different from the lives we were living outside of rehab. It made me somehow feel hopeful that someone who had experienced such challenges could still see beauty and simplicity in the world.

"I love it," I said softly and we continued to smoke and look up at the sky.

Before we all knew it, we were graduating. Everyone's sobriety seemed solid so the idea that 97% of us would fail secmed impossible. But we would learn the harsh truth soon.

I moved into a sober living house where I shared a run-down room in a renovated 1960's era motel with a young guy whose sobriety didn't seem very sustainable. He was using Kratom regularly, a southeast Asian leaf which is ground up into a powder and has opiate-like properties. However, it is legal and only shows up in urine tests unless it's tested for specifically which our place didn't apparently do.

Five AA meetings a week were required, as were nightly check ins including a breathalyzer, and weekly urine tests. Most of the twenty guys in our house had gone through New Frontiers rehab so I knew almost all of them. I also was given the restriction that I couldn't date or be seen with any women. Apparently, my therapist had told the house manager about my other addiction. At the time, I didn't think it would be difficult to comply.

None of us could understand the statistics that we had been told about relapse until John left one night. In the middle of the night, he was gone. No one knew where he had gone and we were all surprised as he regularly went to meetings, had a sponsor, and even a few sponsees. It was all we could talk about in the smoke pit, where we spent the afternoons chatting about life.

And then Carl and James left a week later. Again, without a goodbye. All of a sudden, this seemed serious and concerning. Then Antonio overdosed on the toilet in his room from fentanyl. There was no trouble getting drugs in the neighborhood where the house was located; all it took was a walk to the parking lot across the street. So easy.

After a month I got my car privileges. While I felt no urge to drink, now that I had freedom with a car, I decided one afternoon to go to the strip club. I just wanted to see what it was like without drinking and didn't think there was any chance of getting caught.

However, I made the mistake of getting a ride home from one of the strippers and she had stepped out of the car to give me a hug. Apparently, the grounds had cameras because the next day the house manager called me into his office.

"We saw you with that woman last night," he said evenly.

I knew anything I said would get me in more trouble.

"I'm going to give you one more chance and if I hear or see anything that makes me believe you are not following the house rules, I'm going to kick you out," he said. "Also, one of the new guys has been struggling with women issues like yours and you should talk with him."

I got up, shook his hand, appreciative of another chance, and headed back to my room.

The next day I took out the number the house manager had given me and called Brian.

We had a good chat about our issues and he suggested we go to an SLAA meeting. Sex and Love addicts anonymous. Unless you've gone through it you wouldn't realize that there are at least three groups for people dealing with sex and intimacy issues. SLAA was appealing because it was inclusive of people like me. Those who were basically love addicts with intimacy disorders, looking for validation through others' affection.

While I had dedicated myself to sexual sobriety: no porn, strip clubs, Tinder, sugar babies, and even being around women in general, all addicts have an Achilles heel; that one temptation that is the last to go. Mine was Desi, the 20-year-old from rehab, and when she called one evening (ironically the night before I was going to an SLAA meeting) I answered.

"I'm getting kicked out of my halfway house," she said evenly.

"Why?" I asked.

"I was misusing my meds," she admitted.

"The Neurontin?" I asked, knowing that the mood stabilizer was also used at higher doses for a high.

"Yea," she admitted. "I don't know what to do."

I quickly jumped into my savior, intimacy-depleted, love-addict mode. It was comfortable, like a warm sweater. They say that the dopamine release in the brain for addicts using is 100x more than any day-to-day activity, and you can feel it when it's experienced, along with oxytocin (the brain chemical of belonging and being nurtured). A tough combo to resist.

"I'll meet you by the Starbucks near your halfway," I said automatically without even thinking of the ramifications if I was seen by anyone who worked in our house or the rehab center.

An hour later I was sitting with her at an outdoor table. She was vaping (I don't know of an addict who doesn't vape…) and her duffel bag with her belongings was on the ground next to her.

"What are you going to do?" I asked.

"Probably go back to Colorado," she said, blowing the vapor into the warm breeze.

"You know that's a terrible idea," I replied knowing that was where her abusive and neglectful family lived, let alone where all her "friends" were addicts and dealers. She herself had apparently been one of the largest fentanyl dealers in the area.

"I don't know what else to do…" she trailed off.

"How about I get an Airbnb for you for a week," I paused, "just so you have time to get a job and plan your next steps."

In retrospect, it was a terrible idea. So many times, helping addicts is just facilitating and enabling them but it's so difficult for another addict to see that, especially a love addict in the throes of their addiction.

So, I got her an Airbnb that night, and the next morning the house manager called me into his office.

"Where is she?" he asked.

"Who?" I replied having no clue how he could know about my contact with Desi.

"You let her use your phone to call her dad in Colorado and he called the rehab to see what was going on," he said evenly.

"Shit," I replied.

"So, the only way you can stay here is if you give us her location," he continued.

I knew he wasn't joking and part of me realized that it was for the best for Desi if she went back to rehab before something worse happened to her.

I went ahead and gave the location and went back to my room and waited.

A few days passed and I had heard no news of what happened to her. My friends from the womens' halfway told me she wasn't there and the house manager wouldn't give me any information. I tried to move on (after a small relapse with Janice, after all I had the Airbnb…).

I attended AA and SLAA regularly, got a sponsor in each group, and began to look for a job.

It had been a month since I had last seen Desi at the coffee shop when the house manager called me into his office.

"I'm sorry to tell you this but Desi overdosed," he said quietly while trying to maintain eye contact.

I was silent. "What happened," I asked.

"She left rehab and headed back to Denver," he started, "and her dad found her dead in her bedroom, on the floor, with a foil pack of fentanyl next to her."

I felt myself tearing up. While I don't cry often it was just so sad to imagine her in her parents' house, making that decision to use again, alone.

"I knew you were close to her and her dad appreciated you trying to help her and wanted you to know," he added.

"Thank you," I replied and then turned and walked back up to my room.

19) SOBRIETY-

Looking back, Desi's death was my turning point. There was something about her that I couldn't let go. The brutality of her upbringing, her resilience, the hope, then the hopelessness all swirled within and while I had known others who had died, her death continued to reverberate. I began to use it as a motivator to stay sober. It helped that we had ended up getting the smiley face tattoo on our inner ankles and every time I saw it the irony of the iconic image of happiness was so powerfully juxtaposed with her reality.

Like any addict's story, getting sober is not very interesting. It's just a matter of doing the next right thing, not using, going to meetings, and talking to your sponsor. I started to spend more time with sober friends from meetings and began to even like the group trips to the movies or the golf course with men my own age who had experiences similar to mine. We all knew what would happen if we went back to our old lives and none of us wanted that.

Of course, there are still times that I miss my old life. But a quick look at the happy face on my leg quickly brings me back to my reality, Desi's reality, and the reality of every addict. We need to be completely sober every day, forever, or the addict in our brain, forever waiting, will pounce, and we will die.

The irony was that it wasn't family, old friends, lost jobs, jail time, or hospital visits that motivated me. Finally, it was the realization that I was powerless over my addiction and that actions had to be taken daily to maintain sobriety; a daily reprieve contingent on the maintenance of my spiritual condition.

I've been sober for a year now and I am blessed with better health, a clearer mind, new friends, a new job and a deeper and more meaningful relationship with my kids and siblings. Do I regret the lost wages, pain that I caused to those I loved, legal fallout from my behaviors? Sometimes. But I'm happy with where I am and hopefully, I can keep it going. One day at a time.

Made in the USA
Las Vegas, NV
19 December 2024

14950033R00059